MW01241383

Stories

Told From An Old Oak Stump On Spruce Creek

W. Gene Hughes

1st Place, Top Overall Winner of the
Rockfish River Valley Writers Contest
2020

ISBN-9798642958858

Edited by Wayne H. Drumheller, Editor, Host and Founder
The Creative Short Book Writers Project
The Rockfish River Valley Writers
"Old Winter Green Days" Writing Contest

Authors Disclaimer

This is a work of non-fiction. All stated or implied facts are true and are attributable to historical sources, evidence and data, including documentation developed through interviews, letters, emails and notes to the authors. All statements which cannot reasonably be interpreted as stating actual facts about persons are statements of opinion, inference and suggestion. Further, statements that are relative in nature and depend largely upon the author's viewpoint also are expressions of opinion.

CONTENTS

INTRODUCTION

When I was growing up on Spruce Creek storytelling was an art form though none of those old boys would have admitted it. Most every grownup on Spruce Creek would spin the most outlandish tales and swear that it was the good lord's honest truth. They chewed tobacco and when they spit it created a dramatic pause that you dared not interrupt.

My father, Tucker Hughes and cousin Owen Napier would swap stories underneath the old oak tree at the end of Owen's driveway. Owen would squat down like an Indian, chew tobacco, and spit through his knees. Tucker could not sit like that so he sat on a stump. They would tell stories for hours.

I always remember those days and in my travels, I met a lot of storytellers. Some told the truth and some did not. I have tried to tell the truth in my stories because most times the truth is more entertaining, but there will always be those who are skeptical.

Before the Wintergreen Resort arrived in the early seventies local families made up of Hughes, Napier, Coleman, Campbell, Davis, Phillips, Rittenhouse, Small, Meeks, and McGann had all been living in the South Rockfish Valley. Most of these families arrived at Jamestown in the 1600s and gradually moved westward until they stopped in the Rockfish Valley. I think most of the descendants thank the Lord every day that their families stopped in The South Rockfish Valley.

I have always told stories. While aboard the ship all the sailors would try to outdo each other. The country boys would always win.

I hope you find this book fun and entertaining.

In this introduction, I would like to name the folks From Wintergreen that served Virginia and the United States in its military and dedicate this book to them.

Hawes Coleman, Walker Coleman, Steve, Coleman, Sam Coleman, Hayward L. Dameron, Arthur Drumheller, Artie Drumheller, Eddie Drumheller, Freddie Drumheller, Wayne Drumheller, Hal Ewing, John Wills Harris, Jim Harris, Kaolion Harris, Booze Harris, Toby Harris, Little Ray Harris, Jack Hughes, Little Wirt Hughes, John Hughes, Mitchell Hughes, Bland Hughes, Webster Hughes, Clay Hughes, Richard Hughes, Gene Hughes, Donald Hughes, Beau Napier, The Hatter Family, Big Andrew Hickman, Tony Marshall, Diana Marshall, John Jacob Meeks, Judson Phillips, Henry Rittenhouse, Jack Truslow Jr., Zackariah Phillips, Grady Hughes Wortham

Gene Hughes

Dedication

This book is dedicated to the many friends who have come to the "Old Winter Green Days" festival near the Rockfish Valley Foundation-Natural History Center and the Stoney Creek "Farmers' Market" at Nellysford and taken the time to listen to my stories and laugh, even if they have heard them before. One of them was Ted Hughes who lost his battle to cancer a couple of years ago.

A Spruce Creek Boy Meets The World

The marines were all right out of boot camp which means they were
very gullible, falling for any joke or prank.

It was in June of 1965 that I felt the pull of a different
world out there. My father had passed away in June of
1964. We had been very close and I felt lost without him. I
was living at home with my mother Doris Marshall
Hughes. There was little in the way of work in the Rockfish
Valley. The factories in Waynesboro were out of the
question.

One of my cousins, Little Ray Harris was in the Navy and
had been for almost twenty years. Little Ray and one of his
buddies who just happened to be a Navy Recruiter stopped
by one day. They told tales of how great the Navy was. It
didn't take much to convince me so I took the test right
there on the kitchen table while Little Ray and the recruiter
drank coffee. After I finished the recruiter barely looked at
it and said you passed. By then I was ready to sign up.
They had conned me right in.

 The Recruiter put me on a bus to
Richmond where I had a physical, took
more tests, got sworn in and given a train
ticket to Great Lakes Naval Training
Center, Illinois. Boot Camp was not as
advertised. I expected it to be the hardest
thing I would ever do. It was no worse
than High School Physical Education
class under Coach Sherman League. The hardest was
swimming. I would never become a good swimmer. But
then very few of the old drowned sailors could swim.

Upon completion of Recruit Training, I received orders to
the USS Suffolk County LST 1173 otherwise known

affectionally as the Suffering Suffolk with a side trip to the Assault Boat Coxswain School at Little Creek Naval Amphibious School. At the Coxswain school, we learned all about how to handle landing craft during an Amphibious Landing such as D-Day. Little did we know at the time that Soldiers and Marines would be landing in Vietnam by Jet Airplanes. I liked that school and am glad I was sent there because the training helped a lot later on in the Coast Guard.

I spent four years aboard the Suffering Suffolk. The mission was to take Marines to Puerto Rico and Panama where they were trained in jungle warfare and amphibious operations. For us sailors, it was a great time. The marines were all right out of boot camp which means they were very gullible, falling for any joke or prank.

My favorite prank was the Mail Buoy Drop. The way it worked was a couple of sailors would go to the fantail where the Marines would be sitting around talking and cleaning their weapons. The sailors would be discussing the fact that a mail ship would be dropping our mail off on a mail buoy tonight. The problem was that the seas were so rough that our Radar would not be able to pick it up. The old man had issued an order that a Mail Buoy Watch must be set using volunteers only. You can imagine how that news hit those young Marines waiting for letters from home. They were demanding to be picked for a watch. The Watches were divided into two hours increments, dressed in as much foul weather gear as we could get on them and issued binoculars. The watch was then taken to the bow and told to keep a sharp watch for the Mail Buoy. We usually could get three nights out of this before some old salt Sergeant told them it was a joke. Feelings were a bit dicey for a while after.

Four years of cruises to the Caribbean and Mediterranean

kind of got boring along with the drinking and general hell-raising that comes with being sailors during the waning years of sailors just having fun. Most trouble we got into had a command blind eye turned unless someone got hurt or destroyed property.

Towards the end of my four-year tour, I was told that my enlistment had been extended by one year. Orders had been cut sending me to Earle Ammunition Depot, in Northern New Jersey. When I asked the reason for an extension of enlistment the yeoman said that some sailors have to do five to get four cause they goofed off at least a year. Must have been yeoman humor.

Two things happened that year in New Jersey. This was 1969 and a friend called me about a great music festival called Woodstock was being held in New York and did I want to go. I said Hell Yeah I'll meet you there. Being a sailor and at sea, for the last four years, I didn't know much about getting high with drugs and wasn't interested. Greg Cassini and I loaded up my car with beer and vodka. We were ready for an adventure.

It started raining as we got closer. My car was a convertible and the top stayed down. We were drunk, wet, and utterly miserable. Even though I have a real spotty memory of that weekend I still maintain that I had a grand time.

The other thing that happened that year was that I connected with my Uncle Russ Marshall who lived not far from my base. Traveling with Uncle Russ was an education on the shady side of life for an old country boy from Spruce Creek. He taught me what it was like to live off his wits during the twenties, thirties, forties, fifties, and sixties. I thought of Uncle Russ more as a friend than an Uncle.

Uncle Russell Marshall (The Wonderer)

When Russ returned to Winter Green his parents were overjoyed. He promised he would stay home and be a good boy. That was a promise Russ could not keep.

Uncle Russ was born in 1908. From the time he learned to walk he was hard to keep up with. When his mother or sisters turned their backs he would disappear. They were always looking for him. Russ could not stand being in one place very long and he was a constant worry to his mother.

When the wanderlust hit especially hard in 1922 he was fourteen years old. Russ had listened to all the local men tell stories of their service in World War I. His older brother Tacitus had been a victim of Chlorine Gas in the trenches during the Argonne Meuse Offensive. To Russ, this seemed like a great adventure.

 Russ ran away from home and made his way to Richmond. In Richmond, he somehow found the U. S. Marine Corps Recruiting Office. Russ was a big kid for his age and he had a grown-up way about him. He was able to convince the Recruiting Sergeant that he was eighteen. Russ was sworn in as a U. S. Marine Corps Recruit. He was issued a train ticket and ordered to report to the Training Center at Parris Island, South Carolina. The Great Adventure turned out not to be what Russ had envisioned after a few weeks at Parris Island. When he admitted his age the Marine Corps released Russ. He was given a severe talking to, and a promise he would be accepted on his eighteenth birthday. Russ was given a train ticket and told to go home.

When Russ returned to Winter Green his parents were overjoyed. He promised he would stay home and be a good boy. That was a promise Russ could not keep. After about six months Russ left home again. It was seventeen years before his family saw or heard from him again.

In the nineteen sixties, Russ and his two lady friends were driving from Florida back to New Jersey where they lived and as they were driving north on I81 Russ noticed an exit for Stanton Va. He commented to the ladies that he had been born just east of the mountain. They talked him into returning home to visit his family.

In 1968 I was transferred to the Naval Ammo Station in Northern New Jersey. While stationed there Uncle Russ contacted me. We were not very far apart and I spent a lot of time with him. He liked me to drive him to the horse race tracks as he was an avid gambler addicted to the ponies. Russ owned a Lincoln with the trunk set up like a bar. He drank Four Roses Whiskey. We would stop whenever he wanted a drink. The police there knew him and would stop for a drink themselves. He knew everybody it seemed.

Russ loved to talk about his life and the adventures he enjoyed. Needless to say, he did not return to Parris Island on his eighteen birthday. When he left home the second time after the Marine Corps Russ drifted south working on farms, doing odd jobs, anything to keep moving.

Prohibition lasted from 1920 until 1933. For a young man looking for adventure, this was it for Russ. He took to smuggling whiskey as if he was made for it. New Orleans was a great center for the smugglers. It was a party town. What local law that existed was bought by the smugglers. The few Federal Law Enforcement Officers were helpless.

Russ got in with a group who would take small boats through the bayous to the mouth of the Mississippi where  they would meet mother ships from Europe loaded with alcohol products for New Orleans and the U. S. Market. After many boat trips, Russ was offered a job Driving Whiskey north to Chicago and Detroit. Moving smuggled whiskey by road was much more dangerous than by sea but Russ loved the life. He made a lot of money but he spent a lot.

While in Chicago Russ found that smuggling from Canada was a lot easier than bringing it up from the Gulf. He quit working for the New Orleans people and started bringing in whiskey from Canada to Chicago and Detroit. Russ was pretty smart about this and soon realized that he was getting too well known. It was time to find another interest before the inevitable happened and the law caught up. Russ had no wish to spend time in prison.

As a smuggler, Russ had met and made friends with dockworkers and sailors on the waterfront in Chicago. He asked around and found a berth aboard a Great Lakes collier shipping coal to ports all around the Great Lakes. Aboard that collier was a Boatswain named Iron Mike McNeal who Russ had known from his smuggling days. He and Iron Mike had gotten regular jobs. They became running mates. There was no bar or dancehall safe when Russ and Iron Mike were ashore.

In 1939 or 1940 Russ came home to Winter Green after being gone for seventeen years or so with no word of where he was or if he was even alive. The family was overjoyed but there was a small problem, he brought a wife. He also had no job or visible means of support but seemed to have no money problems. Russ bought a piece of land at the foot of Stony Creek Road and hired Hawthorne Quick to build a fieldstone house for him and his bride Evelyn which still stands today.

Russ was the kind of guy who got along with everybody. It never occurred to him that his family would not like his wife. His mother, sisters, female cousins and women who weren't even kin to him could not stand his wife. I asked my mother one time what the problem was and she couldn't answer. No one ever knew why but they knew they didn't like her.

Things got so bad between Evelyn and Russ's female side of the family that when WWII started Russ decided that he need to contribute to the war effort. Due to his experience with the Marine Corps and the fact that military discipline was not his cup of tea Russ had to consider alternatives that would allow him to do his duty. Russ spent the war years working in the Baltimore shipyards.

After the war, Russ disappeared from Winter Green again and was not seen until the late sixties when he and his two lady friends were driving up the valley and they talked him into going home. To my knowledge no one asked about Evelyn nor did he tell anyone what happened to her

When I first starting spending time with Russ in New Jersey he was not very talkative about his life but after he got to know me we became close and talked more about his life. After WW2 he moved to North Jersey and met some of the folks that he had known during the Prohibition Wars. They had gotten into construction and were running the unions. It was just the kind of thing Russ loved. He kidded the danger and adventure.

I spent two years in northern New Jersey with the Navy and

all my spare time was hanging around with Russ going to bars and restaurants, meeting his friends and generally having a grand time. I learned a lot from Uncle Russ. I think the most important thing he taught me was to live the kind of life you love but be prepared to take the consequences.

Uncle Russ finally was allowed to retire from the life. He took his two lady friends and lived honestly for a few more years in Florida. Having never been arrested he died with a clean record.

A Spruce Creek Boy Decides His Course

I took a stab at civilian life and found it wanting to my taste.

After five years in the Navy, I received my discharge and came home. I had no idea what I wanted to do. I had spent a lot of time talking to Uncle Russ who saw the world as his oyster and he was convinced you could just muddle through doing whatever you wanted. He was a lucky soul because he did just what he wanted. My older brother Grady had the same attitude and tried to convince me that I should hang with him and his friends the Critzer Brothers doing whatever it took to make a dollar the easy way.

The sailor's life is not hard to get used to. I rather enjoyed life aboard ship. A ship's company is truly a band of brothers, a family as it were. The ship is the mother providing a place of safety, food, a feeling of being needed and protected. The Captain is the father providing leadership, knowledge, discipline and a good example. Anyone who has ever served aboard a Naval Ship will understand what an honor it is to be accepted as a crew member of a U.S. Naval Ship.

I took a stab at civilian life and found it wanting to my taste. The only thing to do was call the Navy Recruiter only to be told that the Navy was not shipping over my rank and rate at that time. Plan "B" was to call the Coast Guard. This was on a Thursday morning and the Coast Guard asked if I could be in Long Beach Ca, by Monday morning. I was told not to pack anything and be in Portsmouth, Va. by Friday where I would be sworn in, issued a seabag, and given a plane ticket to Los Angeles, Ca. My orders were to

9

report aboard the Coast Guard Cutter Glacier getting underway for a six-month cruise to Antarctica (In those days we called it a cruise, not a deployment) on Monday morning.

To try and compare the Navy and the Coast Guard is just  not possible. The only similarity is the fact that they both operate on the ocean. There is a definite line between Enlisted and Officers. That line is called Chief Petty Officers and it is seldom crossed. My first day after getting underway aboard the Glacier, Chief Bianco and I had a conversation concerning the difference between the Navy and Coast Guard. The most important thing he talked about was trust. Trust held the whole thing together. After our discussion, we retired to the fantail where we indulged in a couple of shots of rum which would have been unheard of aboard a Naval Vessel. It all comes back to trust.

During my tour of duty aboard the Cutter Glacier, she made two six month cruises to the Antarctic. The main purpose of our Antarctic cruise was to break a passage through the ice to McMurdo Station in order to get fuel tankers and supply ships in to refuel/supply the Station. Glacier also had to stay on station until all refueling was finished keeping the channel through the ice open. A team of scientists was also aboard studying wildlife and taking samples.

These cruises serve as more than breaking ice into Mcmurdo in that Goodwill is achieved by the many liberty ports visited on the way. To name just a few Hawaii, Tahiti, Samoa, New Zealand (North and South Island), Punta Arenas (Straits of Magellan), Santiago, and Lima. Unlike the Navy where only the Officers are Gentlemen, the Coast Guard considers the entire crew Gentlemen. We received invitations to many different Social Functions. Members of the crew were very much in demand to spend time on the great estates around these cities. Of course, we were all perfect Gentlemen.

These trips South were not all fun and games Working topside in that cold was not easy. Everyone had to be careful of getting frostbite by being properly dressed at all times. That was the worst working conditions I have known but the bragging rights of being at Antarctica were worth it. Another source of pride was rounding Cape Horn at the tip of South America. During this time every man off watch had to be strapped into his rack (bunk). One hell of an adventure for an old boy from Spruce Creek.

These trips also entailed a few old Seafaring traditions. The first was Crossing the Equator which involved a whole day of initiation turning Polliwogs into Shellbacks. There were also initiations for crossing the International Date Line, The Antarctic Circle, Rounding the Horn, and the Arctic Circle. All this may seem just fun and games but in reality, it is carrying on age-old seafaring traditions that bring all sailors an understanding of our history and why sailors first went out on the stormy waters to discover new lands and people. It gives one a feeling of kinship with those who have gone before us.

The four-month cruise to Alaska included stops at Kodiak, Dutch Harbor, and Point Barrow. This was a strictly scientific endeavor as a large contingent of scientists embarked.

As Glacier returned to our home port of Long Beach, Ca. to my surprise and delight my orders were in a mail sack on the pier. When I was called to the ship's office I thought that I had committed some sort of indiscretion as I had never been called in before. The yeoman handed me an envelope containing orders to LORSta Sylt, West Germany. You can imagine my surprise. I didn't know the Coast Guard had a station in Germany.

Sylt is an island about four miles wide by about twenty miles long lying on the German-Denmark border and connected to the mainland by a railroad causeway. A crewman from the station met me at the train. He wanted to stop at his apartment for a beer. We walked in and the first thing I noticed was a beautiful blonde sitting in a chair completely naked with the exception of a gold ankle bracelet. Don't ask how I noticed that. He introduced her as his girlfriend and explained that Sylt was a nudist resort. My orders didn't mention that little tidbit. Of course, things aren't always like they seem. You didn't have to pass a looks test to walk around naked. Some of those naked folks should have seen themselves. I doubt many old Spruce Creek boys have seen those sights.

When my tour of duty at Sylt (Every Coasties dream unit) I received orders to Governors Island New York (every

Coasties nightmare). Governors Island lies in New York Harbor off the foot of Manhattan. At the time it was owned by the Coast Guard. The only way to get there was by ferry which was always a hassle. It was also the home of the 3rd Coast Guard District which meant high ranking brass everywhere.

I was assigned to the SAR/Law Enforcement Station as a Boat Coxswain. The job was to patrol the East River as far as Hell's Gate, The Harlem River, and The Hudson River from George Washington Bridge to the Verrazano Bridge including Staten Island. Governors Island was known to be a not a very popular place to be stationed but I rather enjoyed it. We could take our patrol boats out and stay all day as long as we made radio checks everything was good.

The Boatswain Mate Chief was Chief Torres who was our first line boss. He was the best Natural Leader I met in twenty years of service. I always told him he should have been an Officer. He said that it would be impossible because his parents were married to each other. Chief Torres never got upset. When things got sideways for a Coxswain, the Chief would listen to the story, explain how to fix the problem, what should be learned, and then let it go. He was one of the greats, an example that I tried to follow when I made Chief.

Something was always happening at Governors Island. One

February day a fuel carrier ran into a rock up the Hudson River at Haverstraw Bay. We took an amphibious landing craft up there to haul equipment for the cleanup. The cleanup lasted a month and we stayed at a motel running the boats and helping with anything that needed doing. I remember being told to wash the oil off waterfowl. We had small plastic pools and a mild soap. Nobody told us to keep the birds until the lanolin returned to their feathers. A few were lost due to sinking before we got it right. After that, we built pens to keep the birds in for a while. The Coast Guard will rescue anything.

Chief Torres called me in one day and asked if I would be interested in Patrolling the America's Cup Race at Newport, Rhode Island. Are you kidding me? Patrol the America's Cup with no supervision. We were a three-man crew. I think we were there for about a week. What a party time. This was Ted Turner before Jane Fonda. He loved the Coast Guard and a grand old time was had by all. The only downer was that on the way out of Newport the Radar went down and with our luck and a truly horrendous hangover a real London pea soup fog closed on us. I still maintain I was not lost knowing without a doubt I was somewhere in the Western Atlantic. The Good Lord was watching over us because off in the distance one of the guys heard a Bell Buoy. With that Bell Buoy and a chart, I was able to work out a course from one Buoy to another to get us back to Governors Island. When I told my tale to Chief Torres he opined that it might be good to keep this story to ourselves. No Coast Guard Equipment was lost and nobody hurt. The Chief was happy.

While at Governors Island I had the honor of participating in the planning and implementation of the Coast Guard's part in OPSAIL 76. All Coast Guard SAR units were underway for the entire operation which lasted, I think seven days. The three crew members on each SAR boat took turns sleeping on the boats and eating sandwiches. It was a lot of work but a highlight of our time in the Coast Guard. A once in a lifetime happening, celebrating our countries 200th Birthday.

Chief Torres called us in one day and gives us our orders to the Curtis Bay Yards in Baltimore to bring back to New York a New 41 Ft SAR boat. We left Baltimore in pretty good weather but the further north we got the weather started turning. At Townsend Inlet New Jersey we sighted a small boat trying to come out the channel. When they entered the ocean a bow wave caught them and the boat pitch poled spilling all five passengers into the water. It was lucky that we were on the scene and able to pick those folks from the water. Taking people from the sea in those conditions is not easy but thankfully everybody was saved with no injuries. When we returned to New York the crew asked me to speak to the Chief to see if we would receive any recognition. Chief Torres told me to pass to the crew that his recognition of a job well done should satisfy any Coast Guard Lifesaver. That is what I liked about Chief Torres, good or bad he took it all as part of the job.

My next orders were to Sta, Islamorada Fl. where I was to serve as XPO. The Station had a crew of 30 enlisted, no officers. There was a Chief as Officer in Charge and as XPO I was Second in Command. The crew was split between Boatswain Mates and Engineers with one cook. To be Second in Command is probably the hardest job in the Coast Guard. As Second in Command, you act as a buffer between the Officer in Charge and the crew. You must maintain morale and discipline by being a mentor and by being distant at the same time. You must never ever socialize or maintain a friendship with a crewmember. Be ready at all times to criticize or congratulate on a job well done. I did this for five years only taking twenty days' annual leave during that time.

During my time at Sta. Islamorada Drug smuggling was at its height, Haitians were landing day after day, then to top that the Mariel Sealift started. No breaks for the weary. Of course, there were the everyday Sar cases of pleasure boaters, running out of fuel, heart attacks, mechanical problems and taking on water.

My next unit was Officer in Charge Montauk Light Station (LightKeeper), Montauk New York. The Light had a Double Keepers Dwelling. One side was crew quarters and the other side was Quarters for the Keeper and his family. My Wife Sally loved living there. The kids had the entire tip of Long Island as a playground. The main responsibility was maintaining the Light Apparatus.

As I was the last Keeper it was also my job to plan and prepare for decommissioning. There were around five hundred guests invited. Speakers included the Third District Admiral, The Mayor of Montauk, and various other VIPs.

As a young recruit in Navy Boot Camp, I never dreamed that I would spend the last years of my career as a Recruit Company Commander. Cape May Training Center was my last Unit before retirement. It was also one of the most demanding both physically and mentally. Each company is one hundred recruits. The Commander is with them from five o'clock in the morning till ten o'clock at night for the eight-week training cycle. This means being a father, mother, teacher, preacher, and counselor to a hundred recruits. It takes a lot out of you. I am glad it was my last Unit.

I am convinced that the U.S. Coast Guard is the best organization a young person can join. You can truly be the best you can be in the Coast Guard. I retired in 1988 and still think about it every day. This description of my time in the Coast Guard is only a very brief summary of a story that describes a life of adventure and good times.

USN, USCG, BMC, US Army Civil Service, RET.

MY MOTHER, DORIS (FLAXIE) MARSHALL HUGHES

Mental hospitals have always found it hard to attract employees with the inner strength and will to work with the mentally ill.

Doris (Flaxie) Marshall was born in 1902 at River Bluff on the Rockfish River just across from Elk Hill. Her parents were Gilbert and Katherine Marshall. She had seven siblings. One brother Tacitus was gassed in WWI and died shortly after the war and her sister Grace died of the Spanish Flu in 1918. The rest lived long healthy lives. Doris received the nickname Flaxie as a small child due to the color of her hair which resembled the flax plant, a bright golden yellow.

Flaxie attended the School at Nellysford in the building that is now the Wild Wolf Brewery. She loved to tell the story of her having to go to the mountain field to catch a horse to ride to school. I remembered listening to this story many times. So I walked it off and found it would have been no great distance difference to just walk to school instead of catching a horse. She answered that a Virginian would rather walk four miles to catch a horse to ride than walk five miles. You would have to be a Virginian to understand.

Dr. Everett was the local Doctor that attended the sick and injured at Old Wintergreen. Dr. Everett was a family friend and relative of Flaxie's mother Katherine. When Flaxie turned 16 years old Dr. Everett recommended her for a position at the Western State Hospital in Staunton, Va.

After a lengthy interview by the senior nurse and Dr. Dejarnette (another family relative), Flaxie was hired as a trainee working with mental patients. Flaxie was a tough country girl raised on a farm but she had good manners, learned quickly, and was empathetic toward all the patients. Working with the mentally ill is the most physically, mentally, and emotionally draining of healthcare. Flaxie had a strong personality and was able to provide the care that was expected to be given to the mentally ill of that time.

In the early 1920s, the staff lived and dined on the grounds of Western State Hospital in the Staff Dormitory. On occasion, they would have a Sunday afternoon off when they would walk in Gypsy Hill Park. It was a very demanding job but these girls were tough and used to work on the farm.

Dr. Dejarnette was famous for his treatment of the mentally insane. He advocated the use of straitjackets, numerous types of restraints, and most famously for his introduction of Electro Shock treatments. Dr. Dejarnette has received a lot of criticism for his treatment of the mentally ill, but for his time the treatments were cutting edge. As in most history, hindsight is always twenty-twenty to the fault-finding ignorant.

After her training at Western State, Flaxie was offered a position in Detroit, Michigan. Her duties there included traveling throughout the Midwest as a member of the transport team that delivered patients to the hospital. It was a sad heartbreaking job to remove mentally ill people from their family and home to be placed in a hospital far away. In almost all cases the family had tried to care for these folks at home but finally had to admit that it was not possible to provide this care at home without the entire family suffering. In most cases, the hospital was the patient's final home, never to see their family again. Mid-Western people were farmers and travel was limited. Folks had no means or time to visit a relative in a mental hospital.

Mental hospitals have always found it hard to attract employees with the inner strength and will to work with the mentally ill. Flaxie had what it takes and was offered a job in Chicago where she spent a couple of years and then another couple of years in New York.

While working in New York Flaxie received word that her mother Katherine had become sick and was bedridden. Flaxie's father Gilbert asked her to return home and help care for her mother. Her brothers and sisters all had families and were unable to help. As always the dutiful daughter Flaxie resigned and came home to Spruce Creek.

On Spruce Creek the closest Doctor was at Lovingston or Crozet. Flaxie's return home meant that someone with medical training was close by. She could do almost anything except surgery. Her services were in constant demand. Alec Hughes and his wife Sallie lived on Spruce Creek. They were both elderly and sick. Their son Tucker asked Flaxie to look in on them and give them their medicine and shots. Tucker was quite a bit older than Flaxie and a bachelor. After Alec and Sallie passed away Tucker inherited their home. Tucker and Flaxie married a short time after.

As I small child I still remember going with my mother to see sick folks. When she would administer shots they would ask if it would hurt. She always replied that "The pain depends on You". That got a laugh because I can't remember anyone complaining. Flaxie devoted her life to caring for the sick and raising a family. She was a wonderful mother and a great cook. I have tried to not disappoint her and Tucker.

Tucker and Flaxie were the best parents a kid could have and I still miss them.

The Dream and Thoughts of the Hereafter

In the dream, I had died and come back to consciousness.

I woke up in the middle of the night with the remnants of a dream clouding my mind. I normally don't remember my dreams very clearly but when I woke up the next morning the entire dream came back to me as if I had experienced the incident in person.

I was standing at the entrance to a bridge that stretched so far in the distance that I could not see anything but a bright light far away. Walking towards that light many things went through my mind such as how many sins have I committed in the past 74 years and how bad they were.

When I got close to the end of the bridge, I could see an old long-bearded man dressed in a white robe sitting at a desk under the Golden Gate. I think that this must be Saint Peter so I approach him and ask if this is where I report. He said, "You are at the right place come on in we have been expecting you".

Saint Peter didn't ask any questions or talk about my sins. He just said "Mr. Hughes we are glad you are here, just follow that path until you come to an old walnut tree. That will be your assigned spot for eternity if you want to stay."

I asked "What about my sins? Don't I have to atone or ask forgiveness or something? I know I got some fairly bad sins somewhere along the line."

Saint Peter said "You got some pretty good sins, but yours don't add up enough to waste our time on punishing you. Go on and take that path to the old walnut tree."

After about an hour of brisk walking, I come within sight of a tall old walnut tree sitting at the edge of a cornfield next to a creek. It was a most peaceful looking place and as I got closer, I noticed a group of old men sitting around the tree talking and laughing. I thought that this sure looked familiar. As I got closer, I saw why.

I felt like I was coming home. All the old folks were my Uncles and neighbors that I had last seen on Spruce Creek when I was a child. There was my father Tucker that I called Pappy and all the Uncles and neighbors. Pappy said that Mammy was up at our house cooking supper and we could sit and talk a spell. I looked around and knew everyone. Besides my Pappy and the Uncles, there was old Pete Napier, murdered in a knife fight during a drunken brawl. Pete's brother Owen Napier was there squatting down on his haunches like an Indian, telling stories that would last all week. Henry Campbell was hiding behind the tree in case his wife Marjorie came looking for him. Uncle Bland was whittling on a stick and Uncle John was just watching everything. Of course, there was Uncle Bunk chewing tobacco and telling stories.

I was home.

Pappy told me that I didn't have to stay here. He said that rule was that you could go anywhere that you wanted or wherever you were happiest. Pappy told me that he had of course kept up with me and knew that I had traveled a lot, seen both sad and wonderful things. I should be sure of what I wanted.

All these folks under the walnut tree took time to talk to me. The ones I knew remembered me and the ones that had died before I was born also knew me. I knew that I would be happiest sitting under this old Walnut tree for eternity.

I walked back up to the bridge and told Saint Peter that I would stay with my folks for eternity.

As I pass my 75 years on this earth, I think a lot about what comes after. I do believe something does come after otherwise, what is the point? If my dream is correct and you go where you were happiest, then it will all be worthwhile. If not, then the Lord will work his will. I can only say that I have had a wonderful time. I came from a good family and have done my best to live as I was taught by my Mother and Father.

After that dream, I have very little fear of the hereafter.

The Abandoned Baby

"Somebody just left this baby on your truck, they didn't want it so we will keep him."

The following is a very sad story. I will not use the real names even though it happened many years ago and as far as I know, all the participants have passed away. It began in the mid-1940s and I knew these folks as I grew up. This family was made up of a mother and two sons. I don't remember a father ever being mentioned. Even though it has nothing to do with the story they were not the brightest folks that ever walked out of the hollow but you would be hard put to find a more close loving family than that mother and her two sons.

They lived in an old log cabin in the middle of an apple orchard on the side of a mountain. The boys worked in the orchard which was owned by a local farmer. An apple orchard was a pretty much year-round job. Always something to do. In the winter equipment had to be worked on, then pruning, spraying, thinning, and keeping the grass and weeds down. The boys were always busy. They were grown and had never done anything else. I don't think they even attended school at all. The farmer had taught them to drive so that they could take apples to the market in Richmond. Remember this was in the 1940s and things were different.

The boys heard the other men talking about going to the market and they asked the farmer to let them take a load. On the first trip, another guy went with them to show them the ropes. Everything went well, no problems.

The following week the boys were sent to market again. They found their way to Richmond and the Market. By the

25

time they got the truck unloaded, it was dark and the boys were afraid to try to find their way back so they decided to park on the street and sleep in the cab of the truck.

The next morning they woke before daylight. They stretch and walk around a bit before starting home to the Rockfish Valley. As they walked toward the back of the truck they heard a strange sound coming from the truck body. One boy got up in the body and found a bundle of what he thought were rags. The bundle of rags turned out to have a newborn baby tucked in them. There was also a couple of bottles of milk with the baby. The baby was not crying, just lying there half asleep.

The boys looked around and the street was empty, not a thing moving or a person on the street. Remember this was the second time these boys had been in Richmond. They didn't know what to do. The only source of advice was their mother who was back up in the Rockfish Valley. They put the baby up in the cab and came straight home to ask Mama what to do.

Well as you can guess Mama took one look at the baby and said: "somebody just left this baby on your truck, they didn't want it so we will keep him". They lived in that log cabin with no neighbors and no visitors so it was about two years before anybody else knew they had the baby. When the farmer heard they had the baby he said OK another hand to work the orchard when he grows a bit.

When the child got to school age the farmer made sure he attended the Rockfish Elementary School and was in my class. I don't remember him beyond the 3rd or 4th grade. I think they left the county.

My father told me how he was found.

A Ski Trip Or A Body Slide Down The Mountain

There is no way a sober person would ever consider doing this.

I was stationed at Coast Guard Loran Station Sylt Germany in the early 1970's. The island was a nudist resort in the North Sea just off the border between Germany and Denmark, a part of the Friesen Island chain. Summertime on Sylt was one long three-month party. In summer we worked a half-day and took the rest to hit the beach, drink beer, and watch girls.

The winter was an entirely different story. Long, cold and wet. No girls, just sitting in a bar drinking beer. That's not all bad, but boring as hell. You can drink only so much beer and tell lies until you are bored out of your mind. Young sailors tend to get in trouble when they are bored and drink too much beer.

 In early January of that year, I received a call from a girl I had met on the beach during the summer. We had spent her vacation together and kept in touch. Her name was Ilse. It was time for her Winter vacation and she asked if I would like to go skiing for a couple of weeks in the Italian Alps at Val Gardena. Me, being an idiot said sure I would love to Ski in the Alps. Of course, I forgot to add that I didn't know how to ski.

I had the idea that I would go down a week early and learn to ski. I thought, how hard could learning to ski be. Shouldn't take more than a week to learn and I would have it down pat by the time Ilse and her friends showed. Was I ever wrong?

It took me three days to get there by train. There were several changes to be made on that train trip. I missed them all. Being able to speak German and Italian would have been a great help, but of course, all I speak is Spruce Creek English. Those trains had small compartments to sit in. As we were getting close to the Italian border I went to sleep. While I was sleeping the train made a stop and to pick up passengers. When I woke up my compartment was filled with an Italian family. There were four or five kids, a short skinny poppa, and a rather large momma. You can imagine waking up to that, not understanding a word. Before they got off the train I was one of the family. The momma had a great big basket of food. There was sausage, bread, cucumbers, and other things I could not identify. Poppa had some bottles of wine which he shared by handing the bottle to me after every drink he took. I had to accept, manners you know. One thing about Spruce Creek boys, we got manners. It was one of the best meals I had on that trip.

Ilse had made arrangements for lodging and sent me the address. As I could find no one that spoke English. After a couple of hours of wandering around lost I found a police station. A policeman looked at the address and took me to the right building. The clerk was jabbering away at the policeman and I think it was a problem that I was there a week early. The policeman started talking loud to the clerk and a room was found. A waiter brought a plate of pasta and a bottle of wine to my room. I thought that was supper so I ate all the pasta and drank the wine. A bit later the real supper was brought. Those Italians sure know how to eat.

The next morning I set about learning to ski. Renting skis and buying a lift ticket was fairly easy. I figured that the best way to learn was to watch some other folks and just do what they do. A couple of hours later I thought I had watched enough so I would try it. There was a rope tow set up for beginners. A few hours later after figuring out how to catch the rope tow I was beaten and decided it was time for lunch and a beer and beer. The next day I spent the entire day trying to learn to ski. It was a most embarrassing day. Kids just learning to walk were skiing better than me.

A group of Germans arrived at the pension while I was trying to learn to ski. By the time I got back to the pension, they had been drinking for some time. They noticed right away that I was an American (Those Germans are brilliant). Pretty soon we were all the best of friends. We had a hearty supper of wurst and beer. Everybody was having a grand old time.

Who came up with the idea I will never know but all of a sudden we are getting our coats, hats, and gloves preparing to go outside. It was dark and I had no idea what was happening. After walking a ways we came to a gondola ski lift and everybody was handed a round, concave, plastic disk with holes on the side. We all got on the gondola and started up the mountain. I don't know how high we went but when we got off the gondola there were no lights. Everybody got a candle, sat down on the disk and off we went. There is no way a sober person would ever consider doing this. It seemed we went straight down aiming for the village lights. I figured that I was done for. There was no way I would land at the bottom in one piece. I ran into rocks, trees, brush, you name it. I felt like I had been hit by an old western mob.

When I got back to the pension all but one was there. One man's wife drug in about twenty minutes later. She was in a real mess and her husband hadn't noticed she was missing. He was chatting up another young lady when the Mrs. walked in. She ordered a stein of beer, walked over and bashed him upside the head with the stein. That signaled that the party was over.

As much as I hurt the next day I had my answer to the lack of skiing ability. I was all scratched up from trees and brush. Limping along was about all I could do. Down the street from my pension was a drug store. They sold me a box of bandages and a set of crutches.

When Isle arrived I explained that my ankle was sprained but I felt I could take the pain until I got back to Sylt. She couldn't understand that I would have to go to Bremerhaven to see an American military doctor. Isle always thought the Americans were kind of wacky any way but she bought the story and I had a wonderful ski trip.

Ilse may have known that I was not hurt but she was ladylike enough to not bring it up. She spoke English better than I and served as an interpreter for the German Government in Bonn.

Before I left Germany I came clean and told her my injury was a fake. She smiled and said she understood. You got to love those German girls.

The Beginnings of the Winter Green Plantation

As a Virginia Militiaman, he mustered, marched, and fought whenever and wherever he was ordered.

Hawes Coleman was born in 1757 at his father's plantation, Pine Forest in Spotsylvania County, Virginia. His Grandfather Robert Coleman had moved from England to the Northern Neck of Virginia in the 1650's.

After a few years Robert's son, also named Robert, moved to Spotsylvania County and established Pine Forest. As typical of the time, Hawes was educated at home by a hired tutor who resided with the family.

His formal education consisted mostly of the classics and mathematics. Included in the education of a young Virginia Cavalier Gentleman were the arts of riding, hunting, shooting, and how to act in the drawing-room.

In Virginia, there was a law that declared all men of good health between the age of 18 and 45 must join the State Militia. Hawes dutifully joined the Virginia militia at the age 18 which coincided with the start of the American War for Independence from Britain. Hawes had no great desire for Independence but as Virginia went Hawes went.

As a Virginia Militiaman, he mustered, marched, and fought whenever and wherever he was ordered. The Virginia Militia was set up to muster and march whenever danger of war threatened. Generally a militia unit was called out for a specific amount of time, usually 90 days.

During the war, Hawes served with many Generals. Two of the more famous were General Lafayette and General Thomas Nelson. He also served at Yorktown under General Washington. Hawes married but his wife developed a fever and passed away just a few months after the marriage. Not long after the passing of his first wife Hawes met Nancy Ann Harris. Nancy and Hawes were married within a few months.

Nancy Harris was from an influential family in Spotsylvania County. Her two brothers had been granted Commissions in the Continental Army. Even though Hawes was from an equal or higher rung on the Social Ladder the Harris brothers looked on him as inferior due to his rank of Private in the Militia during the war. The constant verbal abuse and backstabbing by the Harris brothers brought Hawes very close to challenging both brothers to a duel possibly causing a family feud against the Harris family. Nancy loved her brothers and she loved Hawes. There was too much bad blood between them to forgive or forget. In order to avoid bloodshed, Nancy decided that the only recourse was to remove herself and Hawes from Spotsylvania County.

Hawes had heard that there was land for sale in the Rockfish Valley of Amherst County just a bit southwest Of Charlottesville. He bought a section land of about 400 acres between Spruce Creek and Stoney Creek. In the Southern Rockfish Valley, the Coleman family gave the couple 12 slaves including a cook and maid. With 400 acres and labor to work it, Hawes had the beginnings of a fine plantation. Hawes and Nancy found a house site about a half-mile north of Spruce Creek on a hill with a large flat field behind it and an abundance of evergreen trees. They named the new plantation Winter Green.

To the end of his life Hawes never forgave nor forgot the insults directed to him by the Harris Family but he did give them credit for his moving to Winter Green and turning it into the most beautiful and successful plantation in the valley.

Mr. John J. Coleman and Family

Tho' gentle as a child he was a good soldier.

At the Battle of Fisher's Hill in the Valley of Virginia, fell, mortally wounded one of the brightest and purist spirits whose life and death have illustrated the sentiment that animates the Southern heart. Aylett B. Coleman, in the 20th year of his age, son of John J. Coleman, Esq. of Wintergreen in the Rockfish Valley of Nelson County, Virginia. The night of 5 October 1864 he died at the residence of Dr. Murphy in Woodstock, Virginia, whose wife and family contributed to his every want and watched spirit's passage to another world.

Born in affluence he was entered at the schools of Harrison, Dinwiddie, and others. When the war began he was a student at the University of Virginia. Fully imbued with the importance of an education he assiduously applied his mind to the acquisition of knowledge and his attainments attest to the success of his labors.

Tho' gentle as a child he was a soldier. Before conscription age, impelled by his country's call, he left his native state and was found battling for freedom in Kentucky and Tennessee. At Donaldson he was at the front and withstood the bullets and the storm of battle. In the spring of 1863 he became a member of General Imbodens Staff and with that gallant officer passed through the memorable campaigns of North Western Virginia into Maryland. He signalized himself by his daring, talent, and alacrity in the discharge of all the trusts confided to him.

In 1864 he connected himself with the artillery battery of that amiable and excellent officer, Capt. McClanahan and demeaned himself in such manner as to attract the attention and seized the admiration of the officers and men.

The circumstances of his death, no less than the manner of his life, indicated the character of the man. A few days before the battle in which he was killed, he wrote to a friend on the eve of going to the front as a volunteer with the last artillery piece belonging to his command that he apprehended serious consequences to himself. Yes, with death confronting him he did his duty.

The characteristics of a great nature he possessed in eminent degree: He was noble: All the sentiments of his soul leaned to virtue, not a thought savored of evil. He was generous: His heart was expanded with its inborn philanthropy and the gentle charity of his nature responded to the touching appeals of humanity. He was brave: To him "grim visage war" had "smoothed his wrinkled front" and with death he talked as "friend to friend" for the blessed light of our holy religion illuminated his pathway through the dark and shadows.

Signed by Captain McClanhan, Staunton Artillery

Aylett Breckebridge Coleman, born January 11, 1844, Nelson County and died October 5, 1864, Woodstock, Shenandoah County, Virginia, USA. Wounded at the Battle Fisher Hill, September 22, 1861. Died at Woodstock, VA October 5, 1864.
Parents: John J. Coleman 1797-1869

Violence At Old Winter Green

According to my mother, he was one of the most disagreeable men that ever lived and my mother rarely talked bad about anybody.

Old Winter Green with its Store, Mill, Distillery, Church, Post Office, Magistrate, and Justice of the Peace was a natural gathering place for the surrounding farmer, families, and workers. Saturday was the day most folks showed up at Old Winter Green. Usually by the afternoon after drinking all day at Old Man Gannaway's bar all the young men would be ready to argue and fight. The worst of the lot was a man named Bill Campbell. Bill was an old-time knife fighter but could also hurt a man with his fist. He had beaten or cut nearly every man at Old Winter Green. Bill finally met his end in Waynesboro when a better knife fighter than him left old Bill hanging over a hitching post with his stomach cut opening bleeding to death. It seems that nobody missed Old Bill and most glad to see him go.

Another bad man that lived there was Tom Truslow. It is my understanding that Tom had never actually killed anyone and had in fact lost a few fights. On one Saturday he and Bill got into an argument and chased each other the entire day. Finally, when it got dark, they decided to give up and have a drink at Old Man Gannaway's bar. Tom lived to be an old man fighting every chance he got but he died peaceably in bed.

A cousin of ours named Harry Marshall lived over on Stoney Creek. According to my mother, he was one of the most disagreeable men that ever lived and my mother rarely talked bad about anybody. Even as a child Harry spread fear and terror among the other children in the neighborhood. I am sure that in today's thought he would be considered a troubled child and medicated. Back then he was just a mean kid and everybody avoided him. He only picked people that were weaker than him to make miserable. Most of the grown men in Old Winter Green had to fight him at one time or another.

I remember the day Uncle John stopped by and told us that Harry had been found over in the field back of his house where the Stoney Creek Golf Course is today slumped over a stump dead. It appeared he had shot himself with his own rifle found lying on the ground next to him. The story was told that he used his toe to pull the trigger. Nobody asked how he did that with his shoes still on. Most everybody was glad to see him go and even at the funeral, there was much joy and applause when they closed the casket. I never heard a mournful word said about his passing.

There lived in our neighborhood on Spruce Creek one of the most gentle and well-liked men that I have known. His name was Pete Napier, my father's first cousin. He lived in a house up on Spruce Creek just past John (Rocky Bottom) Phillip's home. Pete had built this house himself when he got married. I think there were three children born to him and his wife. One day his wife packed up the children and left. These things were never discussed around children so I never knew why.

Pete was a hunter, fisherman, and drinker of the first order. It was said that he could grin at a game animal until that squirrel, rabbit, or deer would just walk over and surrender to Pete. He had the fisherman's patience where he could stick his bare hand in Spruce Creek and catch brook trout. Pete could sneak into a chicken house and take eggs from under the hens and they never clucked.

As I noted above Pete was a drinker. Nobody has ever come up with the names but there was a group of people at his house one night and of course, a lot of alcohol was consumed. The next day a neighbor stopped by looking for Pete to do some work for him. Nobody answered the door so the neighbor pushed the door open and found a man named Clyde Thompson passed out on the floor in the hallway. When the neighbor looked in the next room, he found poor Pete in bed with a butcher knife stuck in his body, dead. Clyde was arrested and though he had not a drop of blood on himself he was tried for the murder of Pete. But being as how they were both drunk, Clyde was sentenced to only a year or so in the State Penitentiary.

To this day nobody knows what happened or who all was there that night. Pete who was a friend to all and a gentle soul was killed. And some of us miss him to this day.

In 1900 a man named John Wills Harris bought Winter Green. After John died his children inherited Winter Green. That was the beginning of the decline and fall of the great house of Winter Green. There were four brothers living in the main house at Winter Green, one lived in the barn with his horses and one owned the Winter Green store. They did nothing but drink and fight one another. At night it sounded like a war going on at Winter Green. From my bedroom window, I could watch the muzzle blast at night while the brothers were shooting at each other. My father used to tell me that when I walked down to the store to be careful and if the Harris brothers got to shooting at each other to come on back home. It was nothing to go by Winter Green and see two or three Harris Brothers fighting in the front yard.

As the brothers got older their sister would come down from northern Virginia and take them back home one at a time to care for them until they died. It was they signed over their share of Winter Green for that care. Whatever her reason she got ownership of the whole place.

One of the brothers while living with his sister started getting headaches really bad so his sister took him to a doctor. The doctors examined him and took x rays. After looking at the x-rays the doctor told the Harris brother that he had never seen X rays like this and they would have to operate to find out what all the little black spots were. The Harris brother told the doctor that it was no worry. That he had been shot by his brother for stealing chickens and those black spots were birdshot pellets where he was hit in the head. The doctor was very disappointed. He thought he had found a new disease. As I have said, "It took the Colemans a hundred years to build Winter Green and the Harris tore it down in less than fifty years".

During Prohibition, the Harris Brothers along with one of my Uncles had a whiskey still on Spruce Creek between John (Rocky Bottom) Phillips house and Billy Hughes House. One day some Revenue Agents showed up at the Winter Green Store asking questions. My Grandmother Sally heard about this and sent my father Tucker to warn his brother and bring him back home before the Agents found the still. One of the Harris brothers, Singleton Harris was hidden down the trail as a lookout. Singleton and my father did not get along. Singleton saw him coming and hid behind a rock. When my father passed, Singleton sneaked up and hit him with a tree limb on the side of his head blinding him for life in one eye. Singleton was known ever afterward as the cowardly sneak he had always been. Like the rest of his brothers, he spent all his days with his head in a bottle.

The families of Winter Green were of Scottish and English descent. They were easy to anger and slow to forgive. Some things are never forgiven.

Spruce Creek Lane, Route 627

Private cemeteries of families who lived along or near Spruce Creek Lane include those of the Fortunes, Allens, Hughes, Napiers, Davis', Marshalls, Damerons and probably others.

Spruce Creek Lane stretches from Route 151 at Wintergreen village for approximately three miles before a gate blocks it at the end of State maintenance. (It is paved for only half its length.) The road doesn't approach Spruce Creek until more than a mile from its beginning, but it is still at least another half mile until the creek can be easily seen. From then on the road follows the stream closely till its end. Beyond the gate, it once continued up through the Big Survey property (now Wintergreen Resort) to its Pryors Camp section on the crest of the Blue Ridge.

Spruce Creek starts high on Black Rock Mountain within Wintergreen Resort, below the Laurelwood Condominiums.

In the past, the area around its headwaters was heavily used by Native Americans as well as black bears. The creek itself was called Shamokin or Shoemaking Creek in deeds of the earlier 1700s, but became known as Spruce Creek by 1800.

In 1881, residents petitioned the county for a public road from Spruce Creek to the mill at today's Wintergreen village, where it would connect with the new route of the main highway down the Southern Rockfish Valley. Previously most residents had no legal outlet from their homes to a public road, but had to depend on the goodwill of adjoining owners of private property. Signing the petition were John W. Fortune, Clifton Goode, Ryland Coffey, Eugene M. Truslow, J. Demasters, W.H. Page, C.C. Truslow, Joseph Truslow, James O. Napier, William

R. Napier, and George Truslow.

The earliest property owners along the proposed route who actually resided on their land apparently lived at the very end of today's road as well as considerably beyond. Here lay 245 acres composed of two adjoining tracts on the edge of the Big Survey, patented in 1770 by Rachel Ayres (the only known female patentee in the colonial period) and in 1787 by Samuel Woods. Inherited by Samuel's daughter, Jane Woods Montgomery (wife of Joseph Montgomery of Glenthorne farm), the property was purchased in 1863 by Walker Manley who was the first known owner to make it his home. Shortly after the Civil War, Manley divided it between four different buyers, and three of those who signed the 1881 petition for a public road lived on these parcels. The one living farthest from the present road was John W. Fortune, who was said to have been already occupying a one-room log cabin high atop a ridge on the property. In 1974, the former Fortune property was bought by Donald Faulkner who was instrumental in the founding of Wintergreen Resort, to which he sold part of this tract at the end of the resort's Fortunes Ridge Drive, which takes its name from early owner John Fortune. Over the years, other occupants of various parts of the 245 acre tract have included Ryland Coffey, W.C. Campbell, William C. and John N. Truslow, several Demasters, several Allens, and Saylor Hatter.

The rest of the land on either side of Spruce Creek Lane, lying between the above tract and Route 151, was for years part of several large farms whose owners lived in the valleys along today's Routes 151 and 664...such as John J. Coleman of Wintergreen farm, Dr. Hawes N. Coleman Jr. of Elk Hill farm, the Rodes family of High View farm, and the descendants of Moses Hughes (who had extensive landholdings along Beech Grove and Cub Creek Roads).

Most of this Spruce Creek property was not sold as smaller owner-occupied parcels till shortly after 1885 (although tenants were living on many of them earlier). Fourteen acres on the right of the road about half a mile from the Wintergreen intersection was bought by James O. Napier and until recently still was owned by his descendants. (Slaughter Public School was on their property from 1890 to 1909.) Much of the rest (over 200 acres) was purchased in several parcels by John and Elizabeth Hughes and their children Robert L., Alexander F., Thomas J., and John J. Hughes. Family tradition says the Hughes had been living on part of this land off and on since the mid-1800s. Some of the farms along Spruce Creek Lane bore names such as Meadow Rock, Deer Lick, Manley Springs, Shelving Rock, and Hind Leg Field.

Probably all the road's residents farmed their land and kept animals, but many also engaged in other occupations, sometimes several. As previously discussed, some residents found Spruce Creek Lane at its intersection with Route 151 an opportune location for a store, post office, or mill...people such as Thomas R. Truslow, Alexander F. and Robert L. Hughes, Devereaux and Richard H. Davis, Sydney Bowen, and others. James O. Napier was listed as a miller on his marriage license and had a blacksmith shop on his property, probably in the first part of the 1900s. At one time or another, Alexander F. Hughes reportedly operated a mail route from Afton, a store, post office, licensed distillery, helped run the Wintergreen mill, and served as a local magistrate. His brother Robert L. Hughes was listed in business directories under Saloons around 1890 (was he helping John Gannaway, or running his own?), and as a carpenter/builder and mill operator in 1911. The same year, another brother Thomas J. Hughes was listed as a grocer in Wintergreen, and D.D. Davis as a barber. Gilbert Walker Marshall was said to have run his own distillery. All these lived along Spruce Creek Lane.

Private cemeteries of families who lived along or near Spruce Creek Lane include those of the Fortunes, Allens, Hughes, Napiers, Davis', Marshalls, Damerons and probably others.

Good Old Boys Just Having Fun At Slaughters

Pat Marshall was a young man with an attitude and Bill Campbell was a bad man with a beautiful daughter.

The place called Winter Green (not to be confused with Winter Green Plantation) today was at one time named Slaughters. Slaughter and Fitzpatrick owned a lot of land back in those days up on Spruce Creek. Down there where Spruce Creek Road meets Rt 151 there was a store, Post Office and Grist Mill run by Alec Hughes. There were also four distilleries and a sawmill owned by Old Man Gannaway.

On Saturdays young men and boys hung around Slaughter's drinking, smoking, cursing, fighting, gambling and generally having a fine old time. Bare-knuckle boxing was quite popular, especially among young black men that greatly admired Peter Jackson who had fought James Corbett to a draw. As the owner of the distilleries, Old Man Gannaway ran all the gambling and drinking. He ruled with an iron will and a pistol on his side, nobody crossed Old Man Gannaway.

Law enforcement was provided by Alec Hughes as Magistrate and Peter Davis as Justice of the Peace. Neither had any training in the law but they made up for their lack of knowledge with enthusiasm. Peter Davis would haul in any miscreants to the Grist Mill porch where Alec Hughes would hold a hearing and decide whether it was important enough to refer to the County Court in Lovingston. Rarely was a referral made because the miscreant was usually kin to Alec or a business associate. A small fine of 50 cents or a dollar was levied and that would be the end. Lovingston Court be damned, Alec Hughes ran Slaughters.

Sometimes a case would get out of hand and things would get physical. One Saturday in July around the 4th Peter Davis brought before the Magistrate one Daniel Fitzgerald charged with stealing a coon hound from Billy Dodd. Daniel, of course, denied it but when Billy called the dog it came to him. It would seem to be an open and shut case but when Peter Davis brought Daniel to the Mill Porch for the case to be heard by Alec Hughes a big crowd formed all backing one side or the other.

Alec brought the hearing to order and everybody quieted down. There was a man in the crowd named Zachariah Hughes, a son in law of Alec. Zachariah was also a good friend of Daniel Fitzgerald. Old Man Gannaway had his still house open and as always on the hearing day, everyone had imbibed a few drops of Gannaway's best. Zachariah got up near the porch and started to argue with Alec about the case. It was Zachariah's considered opinion that the coon hound belonged to Daniel Fitzgerald. Alec replied that he had to hear all sides of the story before he could decide whether to send the case on to the Courthouse at Lovingston.

Zachariah had been imbibing the entire morning was in rare form. This being the in the years before WWI when Kaiser Wilhelm was the bad boy of Europe, the worst name Zachariah could come up with to say that Alec was acting like Old Kaiser Bill over in Germany. This lit the crowd up in a political frenzy.

Alec always wore stovepipe boots. He was standing on the mill porch which brought his boots to about chest high on Zachariah. Alec brought his foot back and kicked Zachariah in the jaw. That took Zackariah out of the discussion and broke his jaw. The crowd in front of the all got to fighting, kicking and cussing. It was a major brawl where only one got hurt real bad and that was Zachariah.

Men spoke with pride of their participation in the brawl with great pride for years afterward.

During the fight, Billy Dodd and Daniel Fitzgerald were standing at the back of the porch. They got to discussing how difficult it was to find a good coon hound, that it might be that as they lived so close, maybe it would be a good idea to hunt together and use the same hounds. The case hearing was forgotten, never to be brought up again.

Another hearing case that I always thought showed a lot of judicial wisdom on the part of Alec Hughes was an incident between my Uncle Pat Marshall and Bill Campbell. Bill Campbell and his family lived in a dog-trot log cabin at the head of Spruce Creek that still stands today.

Bill Campbell was a very bad man. He drank all the time, never worked, and was cruel to his family. Most everybody steered clear of Bill. He carried a big, razor-sharp, fighting knife all the time and would not hesitate to use it when in his mind he had been insulted.

Pat Marshall was a young man with an attitude and Bill Campbell was a bad man with a beautiful daughter. Pat decided that he wanted to court Bill's daughter. Pat walked up to Bill one day at the mill and said he would be calling on his daughter. Bill told Pat that if he came up Spruce Creek he better bring someone to carry him back.

Pat wanted to court that girl mighty bad so he saddled up his horse and rode on up to Bill's house. When Pat arrived, Bill came out and gave him another chance to leave. Pat refused to leave, Bill pulled out his knife and started to carve on Pat's stomach. After about four slices Pat got away and was able to climb back on his horse.

Bill knew that Pat was a popular young man in the neighborhood. He knew also that nobody liked him so he went straight to see Alec Hughes and explained that he had given Pat every chance to back off. Bill even used his chewing tobacco knife instead of his normal fighting knife.

Alec took the story into consideration and after getting confirmation from Pat about what had happened he decided that the case need not be sent up to Lovingston Court. No good could come of it. Pat learned a lesson and Bill stayed at home taking care of his family for a while.

The Storm

By Wednesday night the rain had become a deluge.

Alexander Fitzpatrick Hughes was born in 1859. His family lived between Woods Mill and Rockfish Depot during the War. His father, John J. Hughes was a farmer.

After the War, a lot of farmers turned their attention toward fruit orchards. Apple and peach orchards seemed to do better on what was called new ground. New Ground was created when the mountains and hillsides were cleared. The flatlands had been worn out by raising tobacco year after year

John J. found some land on Spruce Creek at Manley Springs. It was steep, rocky, and rich soil. Just the place for an apple orchard. He moved the family from the flatlands to that mountainside, cleared the land and planted an orchard of Albemarle Pippins. Albemarle Pippins were very popular due to Queen Victoria's endorsement as the best apple she had ever tasted.

Alex spent his childhood working in that orchard. Apple crops were a year-round operation. Packing barrels were made in the winter, cutting weeds, clearing brush, and pruning was done in the Spring. Early summer was spraying for disease and insects. Late summer and early fall were picking, packing, and shipping. Lots of work even for the children.

From 1865 till 1870 there was very little rain. Drought conditions prevailed throughout Virginia. Livestock died of thirst on almost every farm. Most crops dried up, ruined in the field. A lot of families left Virginia and moved west during those years. Along with the drought, there was the shadow of Reconstruction, to be withstood from an unforgiving Union. Many families could not take it so they abandoned Virginia. John J Hughes considered Virginia as his country and he swore to never give up on her so he and his family stayed. He had faith in Virginia.

The summer of 1870 was especially bad. People were starting to think that Virginia was turning into a desert. Topsoil was being blown away. There was dust everywhere. The streets were Charlottesville were covered in four inches of dust. At Manley Spring on Spruce Creek, the orchard was starting to die. The few apples that survived were only good for making brandy.

On the afternoon of September 28th, 1870, a Wednesday there came a few sprinkles of rain out of the east. In towns like Charlottesville and Richmond people came out on the streets to celebrate. There were singing, dancing, and praising of the lord. All afternoon clouds got darker, the sprinkles got heavier, and gigantic black clouds came from the east.

By Wednesday night the rain had become a deluge. The winds were so strong that horses and cattle, already dying of thirst were blown off their feet. Trees were being torn from the earth by their roots, Buildings were picked up and sat down, planks strewn all over. During that Wednesday night, ten and a half inches of rain fell. The rain continued and by Thursday evening another four inches had fallen.

The devastation was complete. Houses, barns, and livestock were gone. Over a hundred people dead with the possibility of many more unknown. All telegraph lines were down, newspapers ceased to exist for some time, and the mail system could not deliver with all roads and bridges washed away. Country families were on their own. With no medical care, no one knows how many perished when family and friends were unable to help.

John J. lost his whole crop and most of the orchard was torn out of the ground or blown down. No one in the family was hurt. The horses and a few cattle were lost. Most of his orchard equipment was broken or blown away. The land was still there and John J. would rebuild.

Alex was eleven years old in 1870. He and his siblings helped their father rebuild the farm and orchard. Their mother Elizabeth took care of the family with the help of the girls. The orchard became very successful but like almost every family enterprise the children tend to move away on their own. John J and Elizabeth are buried at Manley Spring high up on a ridge overlooking Spruce Creek.

Alex was my Grandfather. He passed away before I was born. My father and his brothers spoke of Alex often. He was very successful in his own right. Alex was an Overseer on the Pharsalia Plantation, a farmer on Spruce Creek, a Storekeeper, a miller, a postal official, and a magistrate. He and my Grandmother Sallie are buried on Spruce Creek.

The Storm of 1870 had a great effect on Alex. It taught him that adversity is just a word. Anything can be overcome and it is a man's duty to survive.

I often think of the past and all that the family endured just to make a day to day living. Living through this coronavirus is a piece of cake when you think of the past.

Nelly's Ford, Virginia. How it got its name.

The roadways of Rockfish Valley were very different in those days.

It seems that the Southern Rockfish Valley has been overrun with newcomers wanting to know every detail of our history. They usually get information on the Hurricane of 1969 and most are satisfied with that. There are a few however who want more. It seems that everyone wants to know the origin of the name, Nelly's Ford. They receive all manner of tales about the name. I doubt there are many left who know the truth. I daresay I may be the only one left with knowledge of the sad tale connected with Nelly's Ford. My father related this story to me many years ago along with the warning that it would upset some folks if the truth got told but I think that enough time has passed and it would have no bearing or bad feeling ere. It's doubtful if any descendants are left.

In the years before the Unpleasantness known as the War of Northern Aggression there lived in the valley a family of means who owned a rather large amount of land, with many slaves, with which he ran a very successful plantation. There were six children consisting of five older brothers and the youngest, a girl. The girls name was Ellen but the brothers referred to her as Nelly from the day of her birth. Nelly was the families treasure and everyone's joy. She was a bright star of the valley.

That summer Nelly turned sixteen. She was by far the most beautiful and the best liked among her peers in the valley. Nelly's long silken hair done up in the fashion of the times, her eyes were a bluish-gray (a trait in that family) and she had a personality that charmed everyone she met.. Her friends and family loved her and she looked forward to a wonderful life.

51

During the late fall a visitor arrived in the valley from Baltimore. He was a relative of a family who lived not far from Nelly's family. This young man was a twenty six year old ship's officer whose ship was in Baltimore for refit. He had been invited to spend the winter with his relatives in the valley.

It was common for families to have parties, dances, and all manner of social gatherings during the long winter days. Having turned sixteen Nelly was allowed to attend these social events as long as she had a proper member of her family as a chaperon. As chance would have it Nelly and the stranger met at one of these functions. No one thought anything of it when they met, talked. and danced that first meeting because after all Nelly was considered a sixteen year old child and the stranger was twenty six and a visitor who would be gone soon. Unknown to the family or anyone but the two lovers a flame was lit that night. Nelly may have been considered a child by her brothers and parents but she was an adult in her own mind and she was in love.

Over the course of that winter Nelly and the young man had many short hurried meetings at social gatherings Nelly and the stranger quietly laid their plan. They would leave during the dark of night in the spring. Ride horseback to Scottsville, get married and take a packet boat down the James River to board a ship for Baltimore. As plans go this was the best they could do as Nelly's family would not take this union lightly as they loved her to a fault and wanted her to have the best. The brothers would have stopped them and given the stranger a good thrashing.

It was decided that they would leave in April. The stranger was able to procure a gentle mare with a side saddle as was the custom for young ladies to ride, and a spirited gelding for himself. At midnight with no moon the stranger arrived at Nelly's home. Nelly came through her bed room window, across the porch roof and down a trellis to meet her love. They mounted and rode off not having any idea of how their actions would affect her family and cost a number of lives.

The roadways of Rockfish Valley were very different in those days. The road followed the Rockfish River east to where the Adial bridge is today. There was a ford across the river and the road went through Gullyville, past the Adial Church and on down to where it comes back to the river eventually arriving at Scottsville.

They arrived at the ford and as it was Spring time the water was higher than usual. The stranger took Nelly's reins and was going to lead her horse across. As stated Nelly was riding side saddle which means her saddle had a hook where her right leg was encased in on the left side of the horse and her left leg hung down with her left foot in a stirrup. She was dressed in the standard riding habit for young ladies which consisted of a long dress, a woolen cloak and a canvas duster to keep the mud from her dress. The horses grew skittish at the sound of high water and as they entered the water, a few feet in Nelly's horse slipped on a rock and fell. Nelly was unable to save herself as she was so bundled up in clothing. Poor Nelly was washed down river where she drowned while trying to reach the bank. The stranger's horse fell also but being a strong swimmer he was able to pull himself up on the bank a ways down river thus he did not drown.

Meanwhile at Nelly's home she did not come down for breakfast. The brothers found tracks in the yard that led to the road. They saddled up and followed. When they reached the ford they found the stranger sitting on the river bank. He told them the story and they searched the river on both sides until they discovered Nelly's body.

In those days in the Southern Rockfish Valley justice was usually swift and left little time to leave it to a judge in the Lovingston Court House which the people in the valley have never trusted till this day. The five brothers took the stranger to a tall oak tree beside the road and hung him in full sight of all who passed. He hung there till his body separated from the head. No church would accept the body for a proper burial so slaves dug a grave in the roadway so that after a few months no one remembered where he was buried.

Sadly the story does not end there. It wasn't long after that Virginia went to war and all five brothers were called to defend her. By all accounts they died as heroes. Two years after the war their father was found lying beside a stump on what is the Stoney Creek Golf Course today with a bullet hole in his temple and a pistol in his hand. The mother suffered from melancholia. She was placed in the Western State Hospital for the Insane and died soon after from what could only be described a broken heart.

The ford across Rockfish River at the entrance to Adial and the small village nearby has been called Nelly's Ford even though most folks have forgotten the reason why.

Walker and Nancy of Turkey Scratch

Walker and Warren were both unable to carry on as soldiers so they left the army during the retreat from Petersburg.

John Walker Coleman was born at Winter Green in the Southern Rockfish Valley during the late 1830's. He was the son of John J. Coleman and the Grandson of Hawes Coleman, veteran of the War of Independence, also the builder of Wintergreen Plantation considered to be the most successful plantation in the Rockfish Valley.

As the eldest son of a wealthy plantation owner, Walker had a childhood of privilege, wealth, and discipline. A tutor was hired and all the children were educated at home in accordance with the customs of the times among the wealthy. Mathematics and the Classical Works were the main subjects. The children were never given nor taught physical work as it was not expected of their class. Walker spent most of his time sitting under an old oak tree reading or riding horseback over the country around Winter Green. During his rides he met many of the local young farm kids and of course developed friendships.

When Walker returned home after receiving his Law Degree from the University of Virginia his father, John J. had a long talk with him. John J. explained that Walker being the oldest son would inherit Winter Green and would be expected to marry into his class.

Walker wanted very much to inherit Winter Green as he looked forward to the leisurely life of a land owner with time to study, read, ride and hunt. He dearly loved to meet with neighbors to discuss politics and have a dram or two. What he did not like was having to marry someone picked by his father. It was one custom of the wealthy that Walker did not agree with.

There was a local man named Joseph Meeks who had married one of the Giannini girls, whose family had come from Italy to lend their wine making expertise to Thomas Jefferson. Joseph had a daughter named Nancy. Walker had met Nancy before he attended the University and they fell in love. John J. told Walker that if he married Nancy he would not inherit, as the Meeks family was not of his class nor would she bring any wealth to the marriage. Walker's heart was broken but being a dutiful son he obeyed his father and did not marry Nancy.

Not far from Wintergreen there lived a farmer named Warren Davis. Warren's farm was not very successful as his land was mostly hilly and rocky. All the good land was taken by the large plantations. Farmer's like Warren did the best they could. Warren knew both Walker and Nancy. Shortly after Walker had informed Nancy that they could not marry, Warren began to court Nancy. They married and had two children. Walker lived at Winter Green. It was thought that he would remain a bachelor rather than marry his father's choice of a bride for him.

At start of the War, Warren joined the army right away. He was assigned to Pegram's Light Artillery as an ostler (worked with artillery horses). Walker and his brother's all served during the war. Walker served with Crenshaw's Battery of Light Artillery under Pegram. It just happened that Warren Davis was assigned to the same battery. When Walker joined Crenshaw's Battery, Warren was already there. They had known each other all their lives. Walker and Warren liked each other. There were no ill feelings on Walker's part about Warren and Nancy being married. Walker had chosen Winter Green over Nancy and that was that.

Towards the end of the war Crenshaw's Artillery was at Petersburg, Virginia. The Confederate Army was in bad shape. The men and horses were starving. Disease was taking a toll on every unit. The soldiers knew that the end was near. Men were bleeding away from the Army and going home. These men were labeled invalids and considered deserted from duty due to disability.

Walker and Warren were both unable to carry on as soldiers so they left the army during the retreat from Petersburg. Warren had gotten so sick that he was unable to walk so Walker liberated an Army Artillery horse to carry Warren. Thus they returned to Winter Green.

After the war Winter Green's fortunes started in a downward spiral. A long drought had set in and of course the labor necessary to the success of a large plantation had been freed and told to sink or swim on their own. Many left but a few faithful stayed on and kept the farm going. With all the problems, John J. decided that as he could not run Winter Green as a large plantation he would divide it among his children. Walker had not married so instead of inheriting Winter Green he was given about 400 acres on Stony Creek that included Shelving Rock, Turkey Scratch, and part of Big Levels.

Walker returned from the war and regained his health. He was physically healthy but still had the ideals of being a gentleman that had been instilled in him as a child. Walker borrowed money from John J. and had a large log home built at Turkey Scratch.

Warren never regained his health. He was sick and bedridden the rest of his life. Nancy had been living with her parents while Warren was away and when he returned they had to leave. Walker needed a housekeeper in his new home so he hired Nancy. Warren and Nancy moved into Walkers home and began her duties as housekeeper. Warren remained bedridden.

A short time after they moved into Walker's home Warren's health took a turn for the worse and he passed away. Walker and Nancy's relationship changed after Warren's death. They went from employer-employee to living together not legally married. The Coleman family and the community at large, of course, decried the situation but Walker and Nancy paid no attention. They lived together and produced four children. From all accounts they were one of the more loving and happy families in the Valley.

When Walker passed away, he was buried at Winter Green and all of the Coleman family attended the funeral. Nancy was one of the last to arrive. The casket had been closed and was made ready to lower away into the grave when Nancy in tears demanded the casket be opened so that she could see Walker one last time. She leaned into the casket and kissed his cold dead lips and said goodbye. Within a year Nancy joined Walker in death. It is no doubt that they dwell in heaven together in final happiness.

At Walker's death each child was named in his will and received a part of Turkey Scratch. To this day there are many descendants of Walker and Nancy in the Rockfish Valley. After many years most members of the Coleman family accepted the offspring of Walker and Nancy as part of the Coleman family of Winter Green.

Winter Green Plantation After The War Of Independence

Due to the Westward movement, Hawes was able to add to his Winter Green holdings.

Upon arriving at Winter Green Hawes and Nancy moved into a small house on the property. After getting the first crop of tobacco planted work was started on the Winter Green House which still stands despite no significant repairs by the present owners since it was bought in 1900.

Tobacco was the main crop and being labor-intensive it required a great many workers. The crop started in the winter when the seedbeds were prepared. Seedbeds had to be placed on new ground which required trees had to be cut and burned over the beds. The fields were then ploughed, harrowed, and rows laid off. This was done in a very precise way as tobacco had to be planted in a hill within a 36-inch square. Planting the tobacco seedlings was very time consuming as the seedling was so delicate. During the growing season, the tobacco had to be constantly hoed and tobacco worms removed.

At harvest time the tobacco leaves were cut and placed in a curing shed where it was cured by a smoking fire. It was then graded and packed in a hogshead (large wooden barrel) then shipped to Richmond for auction. Tobacco was the main money crop but Wintergreen also produced corn, wheat, and lumber.

Due to the Westward movement, Hawes was able to add to his Winter Green holdings. Toward the end of his life in 1840, he had accumulated approximately 12,000 acres from a start of 400 acres. Nancy Ann died in 1809 leaving Hawes with small children to raise alone. A few years later he married Ann Overton of Louisa County. Ann became his wife, a mother to his children and she also brought some wealth to Winter Green. By all accounts, they were very happy. The children were educated at home by a tutor who lived with the family in the manner of most plantation owners of that time.

Sometime in the early 1830's John J took over the responsibility of running the Winter Green as Hawes was getting older and unable to continue to provide the leadership and assume the workload of a large plantation like Winter Green. John J. was the eldest son of Hawes and Nancy Ann.

In 1836 Hawes at the age of 79 Hawes was notified that he was eligible to apply for a pension earned for his service in the War of Independence. Until his death in 1840 Hawes received a whopping $8.00 per month for a total of $384.00.

In the years before the war Winter Green was doing well. Winter Green's labor consisted mostly of slaves and a few poor white families. The slaves were not kept in a quarters like Mulberry Row at Monticello. They lived on individual lots in cabins spread over the entire plantation. Each family was issued meat, cornmeal, flour, molasses, and clothing. They were allowed to hunt, grow vegetables, and raise chickens. Anything not used could be sold by the slaves. The only punishment allowed at Winter Green was a strong tongue lashing by Hawes or John J. Winter Green never had a white overseer. Hawes was a hands-on plantation owner. He believed in explaining what he wanted done and he would inspect after the job was completed. Hawes treated his people well and received their respect in return. Most of the people stayed on after the war and John J. paid them what he could.

John J. and his wife Catherine had six sons, all of

conscription age. After being tutored at home they all attended the University of Virginia. Hawes N. was a Medical Doctor and also built the plantation Valley Mont. Sam, John J. and Walker, and William studied Law. Sam and John practiced law while Walker and William returned to Winter Green after University.

Walker and William had gotten so used to the life of privilege afforded to plantation owners sons and students at University that they were not interested in pursuing their chose profession. They came back to Wintergreen living as they did before university. They chose to hunt, read and attend social events.

At the start of War in 1861 five of the sons answered Virginia call to service. All were privates as their grandfather Hawes Coleman had been during the War of Independence. The sixth son Ayelett was not of age until 1863 when he quit the University and joined General Imboden's Staff at Fisher's Hill where he was wounded while leading an Artillery Battery. He was placed in a Confederate Hospital at Woodstock where he died. His body was sent back to Winter Green where he was buried in the Family Graveyard. The other sons lived through the war and returned home none the worse for wear. The sons all lived a normal life and are buried in the Family Graveyard.

Winter Green started to decline after the War. A long drought occurred in Virginia from before the end of the War until 1870. Tobacco had already weakened the soil and with no rain, the crops were very poor. Corn and wheat also needed a great deal of water. Winter Green could not support the labor that had elected to stay so most simply drifted to the cities or went out on their own. A hurricane-like storm occurred in 1870 that broke the drought but also completed devastated the valley, all of the bridges and roads were washed out along the Rockfish River. Over a hundred deaths were recorded from this storm. No one knows how many deaths were due to the storm but bodies were never found.

John J. would not leave the Plantation to his eldest son Walker due to Walker's lifestyle of self -indulgence and his choice of a mate that John J. did not approve of. He left Winter Green to his daughter Clara. Walker and William lived at Winter Green until their deaths in1898 and 1899. Neither was any help whatsoever to Clara in the running of Winter Green. Clara married Ivanhoe Cabell and moved to his Plantation on the James River east of Lynchburg. Clara never visited Winter Green again.

In 1900 a year after Walker and William died Winter Green was put up for sale. It was bought by John Wills Harris. John Harris was a relative of Nancy Harris, Hawes Coleman's second wife and the mother of his children. John was also a relative of her two brothers that Hawes almost had a duel with. By getting Winter Green the Harris family had a last shot at Hawes.

The Harris family were not the best stewards of the land. From the 1940's through the 1960's the Harris brothers lived there. The house deteriorated into an irreparable condition during their stay. They worked the land just enough to keep themselves in wine and whiskey.

Nine acres beside the house were recently bought by two foreigners who have placed pet donkeys on the property and seem to have the irrational idea that everyone wants to harm the donkeys. A Harris descendant who sold the land to the foreigners retained the house.

It is a truly sad ending to this beautiful jewel of the Rockfish Valley, Winter Green.

Describing A Tobacco Crop In 1801

During late fall the tobacco fields are plowed and left to freeze, thaw, freeze thaw through the winter until around the first of April.

Tobacco is the most widely grown crop in Virginia. It not only provides a return of profit to plantation owners it also acts as a trade product for the country from whence the government draws its operating expenses. Without trade the government would fall.

Around the first of January I find a good piece of land with drainage and rich soil, with plenty of trees around. The men start downing trees and cutting them up into lengths that can be stacked in piles. All of the small limbs and brush are then thrown on the piles for burning in February when the ground starts to dry. The seed beds are about 15 feet by 20 feet. The burning wood is raked back and forth over the beds to burn evenly. Burning the beds are done to ensure that all weed seeds are dead and the ashes are good for keeping the soil soft after being hoed into the ground.

After the burning, the men rake the bed until they are soft and smooth as sand. The seeds are then spread back and forth both ways to cover all of the bed. The men then take off their shoes and walk over the entire bed in their bare feet in order to uniformly push the seeds into the ground.

A few days after planting the beds are covered with a thin layer of cured horse manure. After several weeks a layer of straw is strewn over the beds to keep in the moisture. The beds are then covered with a light sheet of canvas to keep out a fly that is particularly destructive to tender young plants. The canvas is removed as the plants get stronger.

During late fall the tobacco fields are plowed and left to freeze, thaw, freeze thaw through the winter until around the first of April. The fields are then coultered up (plowed with a plow head that breaks up clods). This is a very time consuming process. The harrow comes next and is run over the soil to smooth it out and make it ready for the plant furrows.

Laying off the rows is a very precise job and has to be done by a skilled worker. I always have Daniel lay off the rows He sits up his stakes six feet by six inches and then runs a furrow in the middle six inches. Making the outside of the row three feet three inches for the planting. Daniel always spends a lot of time sighting the stakes with the greatest of pains and walking rigid so that the furrows will not vary a fraction of an inch. Daniel is very proud of his skill in laying off furrows and it is a pleasure to watch him. Daniel has surely taught me a lot about planting tobacco. After laying off the furrows one way Daniel then turns and lays it off the other way making squares three feet by three inches.

Now each square has to be hilled up. All the dirt in the square has to be drawn up into a hill in the middle of each square to make a perfect cone. To give an idea of how big a job this is there are about one hundred and twenty thousand hills in twenty five acres.

To start planting a man has to go ahead cutting the top off each hill forming a flat spot. A worker then drops plants on each hill doing two rows at a time. Planters then follow using a dibble stick to make a hole in each hill and setting the plant after clearing any old soil from the plant root. That makes the tobacco have a faster, healthier start. After about 10 days the grounds have to have the coulter plow go over the crop between rows. Each hill is then worked with a hilling hoe to pull the dirt back up around the plant. This is called skimming the tobacco.

Tobacco is a fast growing crop. If you planted the last day of May it will be ripe the last day of August or the first day of September. The tobacco has to be ploughed at least three times during that time and workers have to hill each plant up after every ploughing.

Along about August the tobacco worms start to attack the plants and it continues till the last plant is cut. The worms have to be removed from the tobacco in a careful manner by hand. They are placed in a bucket and poured onto a fire at the end of the rows.

Topping tobacco is done by breaking the tops off plants causing the plant to sprout more leaves instead of growing up. This requires some skill and knowledge of how tobacco grows. Knowing where to break the top is very important because the plants a very delicate and can be killed easily.

The tobacco is cut and left to lay on the hill so that it will wilt and not break or tear when handled. Plants are then gather into pile of eight to ten After laying for a while longer given a chance to wilt even more they are carried to a scaffold to be hung on sticks. Each stick is about four feet long and an inch wide. Eight to ten plants are placed on the stick. The sticks are left on the scaffold for a few day and then place on a wagon and taken to be hung in the smoke house for curing. After the plants turned yellow fires are started under the sticks to start the smoke curing process. This takes about three days and someone has to be awake and on watch to ensure the plants don't catch fire. The fire flames have to be carefully controlled. When the curing is done the sticks are taken down and covered with straw to keep it from drying out.

In February the tobacco leaves are removed from the stalks and made up into bundles. The bundles are then placed into bins where boards are placed on top with rocks to compress the tobacco down. After a time the bundles are taken to the packing shed where it is packed into hogsheads which are large wood barrels that hold 1,500 to 2,000 pounds of tobacco for shipping. A horse drawn wagon can carry two hogsheads at a time down to Hatton's Ferry to be placed on aboard a batteau for shipment to Richmond.

From Under A Flat Rock Up On Spruce Creek

Dr. Everrett and John Ryland got along just fine until they married the Martin sisters.

During those years around 1900 there lived in the Southern Rockfish Valley two cousins who had always been the best of friends. Charles Everett had attended the University of Virginia where he attained his Doctorate in Medicine. Dr. Everett decided to open his practice in the Rockfish Valley as he had family in the area and there were no Doctors.

Dr. Everett's cousin John Ryland Coleman also attended The University and received a Law Degree. John Ryland returned to the Valley. He practiced some Law but was mostly involved in politics. He served one term in the State Legislature where he gave a less than a stellar performance. His one shining moment was when he dumped a basket full of rattle snakes on the floor of the Legislature. That act pretty much killed his political career.

Dr. Everrett and John Ryland got along just fine until they married the Martin sisters. It so happened that the sisters owned a large amount of land. As is well known where land is involved and Coleman's are involved there will be a problem. Tales were told on each other, harsh words were exchanged. John Ryland was known to have a bad temper and would fight at the drop of a hat.

On that dark day Dr. Everett was at the old Wintergreen Store sitting on a nail keg chewing tobacco, drinking Gannoway's apple brandy, and giving free medical advice. John Ryland rode up, dismounted and entered the store. He spied Dr. Everett sitting on a nail keg. John Ryland said "You will not take my name in vain again" He pulled his pistol and shot Dr. Everett in the chest". John Ryland walked slowly out of the store, mounted up and road away thinking that he had killed Dr. Everett.

The Justice of the Peace, Peter Davis quickly got a posse together and rode after John Ryland. They caught up with him at the bottom of Dr. Everett's Hill. When John Ryland realized that he was being followed he stopped, got off his horse and waited. When the posse road up John Ryland aimed his pistol at Peter Davis and said "Turn back cousin or I will drop you in the middle of the road". Peter Davis and his posse decided that discretion was the better part of valor so they turned back.

John Ryland left Virginia to visit relatives in Kentucky. After he had been gone a few months he received a letter telling him that Dr. Everett had not been killed because he was wearing his stethoscope. Dr. Everett was just bruised a bit. John Roland returned home. Dr. Everett was always a bit wary when John Ryland was near.

World War I Comes To Winter Green

Tacitus was a tad late donning his mask. Enough gas got in his lungs to take him out of the trench but not enough to kill him.

Many Families in the Rockfish Valley had sons drafted into the Armed Forces in 1916, 1917, and 1918. The War in Europe had begun in 1914. The United States had managed to stay out of the War until 1917 when Germany increased its use of submarines and were attacking U. S. Ships in their endeavors to supply England and her allies.

Thomas Jackson Hughes (Named after one of Virginia's Greatest Generals, (Stone Wall Jackson) was born in 1892 To Alexander and Sallie Hughes. Tacitus Marshall (Named by his Grandfather Walker Coleman after a Roman Historian) was born in 1893 to Gilbert and Catherine Walker Marshall.

Living within a half-mile of each other on Spruce Creek and being so close in age the two boys became the best of friends. They both attended school in the one-room school located on the Napier place. Being farm boys they also worked hard. There was corn to be plowed, apples to be picked and some tobacco crops. All of this was labor-intensive. It helped that they were from large families.

All was not hard work. As they grew into young adulthood they were invited to dances and parties. There was something going on every weekend. They learned the joys of alcohol while watching boxing matches and horse races at the Winter Green Store. For Jack and Tacitus, hunting was their greatest passion. Both had horses and foxhounds, also in the higher mountains above Spruce Creek was bear and coons. Wild meat was a staple at both the Hughes and Marshall homes when the boys hunted.

Jack and Tacitus were of conscription age in 1913. World

War 1 started in 1914 with European nations involved. Right away rumors started that the United States would be drawn into the war. It took almost four years for that to happen. Conscription took Jack and Tacitus at the same time.

After initial training, Tacitus was sent to the 116th Infantry Regiment 29th Division, The Blue and Gray, descendant of the Stone Wall Brigade. The Division was sent to France, where as a Private, Tacitus learned a lot about digging trenches, living for weeks unwashed in lice-ridden clothes, and being under almost constantly artillery barrage. In September of 1918, the Division took part in the Meuse Argonne offensive. This was the largest, most deadly battle in American Military history.

In 1915 the Germans introduced Chlorine into WW1 when they used it on French colonial soldiers. By 1918 it was common practice by France, England, and Germany. Sprayed into the trenches it laid low and was a very effective weapon. Even though masks were provided the soldiers weren't very effective. Gas was especially hideous when used at night when soldiers were asleep. To wake up, don a gas mask before taking a breath was almost impossible.

The company that Tacitus was attached had been under artillery fire for three days. Three days on alert awaiting an attack. On the third day when half the company stood down for rest and sleep the Germans launched a gas attack that took out a fourth of the company. Tacitus was a tad late donning his mask. Enough gas got in his lungs to take him out of the trench but not enough to kill him.

Jack finished his initial training and was placed in an Engineer Training Regiment. The Engineers were sent to France where they spent they were used in bridge building, road building, laying barbed wire entanglements, digging dugouts, and building dressing stations. Jack had worked all his life and this did not bother him. He was quite pleased in that the work was not that much different from home.

Jack's unit was building aid stations and digging trenches in the same area of the Meuse-Argonne that Tacitus was ordered. They were not aware of one another. Jack had not been issued a gas mask but as luck would have it he was out of the trench when the gas attack was launched. He did not receive a large dose but it was enough to take him out of the war.

Jack and Tacitus both lived but were unable to work as they had before the war. Their lungs were ruined and both knew they would not have a long life. The families indulged them. They rode to the foxhounds, hunted bear and coons, and attended every dance.

The government opened a hospital in Johnson City, Tennessee for the care of soldiers who had been gassed during the war. As Jack and Tacitus got weaker it was decided that they needed more care than was possible at home so they were sent to the gas victims' hospital in Tennessee. When they died the families were notified. Sallie Hughes and Catherine Marshall took a train to Johnson City and brought their boys home.

Jack and Tacitus were my uncles. Jack was my father's brother and Tacitus was my mother's brother. I never knew either one. They died before I was born. During their short lives, they made an extraordinary impression on everyone they met. Everyone spoke of their kindness, love of the outdoors and their sense of humor.

They did their duty. I wish I had known them.

Hog Slaughtering On Spruce Creek

First, the killing had to be done.

Up on Spruce Creek above Winter Green between the middle of November and the middle of December when the weather was cold enough it would be time to kill hogs for winter meat. This was a farm event that included everyone in the family. Usually, three or four families would get together and do most of the heavy work.

First, the killing had to be done. This job was always allotted to Uncle Bland due to his having been a soldier in the trenches of France during WWI. Uncle Bland was used to it and he was a good shot. Not one to waste ammunition Uncle Bland could effect a kill with one shot between the eyes. Uncle Bland always commented that he hated killing German soldiers and rather it be Frenchmen he killed because they urinated in the streets and ate horsemeat. Uncle Bland loved his horses.

Old Bill was Uncle Bland's horse that he had bought as a colt. Old Bill was a pet. He hated harness and work with a passion. Uncle Bland usually indulged Old Bill but during hog killing time Old Bill had to break down and earn his oats. Old Bill was hitched to a ground slide. The carcass was wrestled onto the ground slide which usually took about four men. Old Bill was gently coaxed into towing the ground slide down to the creek behind Uncle Bland's house with a great amount of cursing and yelling by Uncle Bland who didn't mean a word of it and Old Bill knew it. This went on all day as the hogs were brought one by one to the creek. Old Bill receiving an apple every trip.

Down by the creek, there had been built a large wooden platform with a long metal tub beside it. The hog was drug up on the platform and a gambrel stick was placed between the hocks of the hogs hind feet. A pole had been placed high above the platform to hang the hog from by the gambrel stick. While hanging from the pole the hog's throat was cut and it bleeds out in a bucket to be saved to make blood sausage. Blood sausage is a very old form of sausage made by cutting pieces of meat up in the blood and cooking it till it congeals. "Wonderful".

After bleeding out, the hog is gutted by cutting him from throat to tail and removing the entrails including the liver, heart, and lungs (lights). By custom, the entrails are given to the colored help. In this case, it is Viola Stuart one of my favorite people. She would clean the entrails in the creek and take them home for her family to eat as chitterlings. No one would admit it but she also received a ham, shoulder. and sausage. Customs were different then.

The hog was then placed in the metal tub of hot water. This served to clean the meat and it also loosened the hair. An old Mason jar lid or if available a proper hog scraper was used to remove the hair. The hog was then rehung on the pole and allowed to hang overnight to cool down thus making it easier to butcher.

My father would always take the brains home to be fried with eggs the next morning. We always looked forward to that. Just thinking about it makes me homesick for those days. After breakfast, the hogs had to be taken down and cut into manageable pieces. Some would be salt-cured and some would be smoked.

Salt curing involved soaking the meat in salt and rubbing it into the meat. A hole was punched down by the bones to push the salt in. It was a time consuming and labor-intensive. The salted meat also had to be soaked to remove the salt for it to be fitting to eat.

Smoking was by far the best way to preserve meat. Hams, shoulders, ribs, and jowls (old English for jaws) were all smoked but by far the best was sausage. Sausage was ground up pieces of trimmed meat and fat placed in a cheesecloth tube then hung in the smokehouse.

Lard and soap were two other items mad from hog fat but I can't remember exactly how because they were done by the womenfolk.

Hog killing time was hard work but as my father used to say "This winter when the snowbirds are flying you will be glad to have a jowl to cook with your beans."

Uncle Bland's Porch

Uncle Bland was the kind of young man that made a perfect soldier

Up there on Spruce Creek above Winter Green during the long hot days of summer when I was a child, I would visit with the Uncles who lived along Spruce Creek Road. There were very few other kids to play with and spending time with my Uncles, listening to their stories and their life's view was better than any amount of playtime with other children. One of my favorites was Uncle Bland Hughes. He was always entertaining. Uncle Bland loved to tell stories about his service during World War 1, life in general and politics.

Uncle Bland was the kind of young man that made a perfect soldier. He had grown up on a farm with seven brothers and four sisters. The farm was a mountainside apple orchard which required year-round care. His father Alexander F. Hughes was also the Winter Green Magistrate, grist mill owner, and a general store owner. He was also the Winter Green postmaster. Growing up, Uncle Bland worked constantly. There was always work to be done on that farm. Alex Hughes was a hard taskmaster. The eight sons worked from daylight to dark six days a week. This was the kind of life the Army would have loved all of its recruits to have. Hard work and instant obedience ground into them.

Uncle Bland's entrance into the army was in his words "less work but it was not Mammy Hughes Cooking". He always talked of the army as his life great adventure. Uncle Bland was of course assigned to the Infantry as most of the farm-raised boys were in those days.

In those days communication was very poor so the commands had to assign runners. With Uncle Blands background as a farm boy in these Virginia mountains, he was a fast runner so he volunteered. He liked that job because it got him out of the trenches where he could move around, get to know people and be considered trustworthy. He hated to be cooped up in the bottom of a trench so running messages was just the job for Uncle Bland.

Uncle Bland would never shed tears but his eyes would get a bit misty when he talked about the refugees he would see along the road as he ran. He spoke of families slowly walking nowhere in the rain and mud with no belongings except the clothes on their back. Old folks and children lost, without food or a roof to get under out of the rain.

The suffering that affected him the most I think was that after an advance on enemy positions there would be many wounded and dead artillery horses. The main concern was taking care of the wounded soldiers and removing the dead. Horses were left to suffer or die on their own. These were mostly artillery horses. There would be horses harnessed together, one wounded, one not. No one to cut them loose.

Uncle Bland was at headquarters one day waiting for a message when an attack was launched. He knew that horses would be wounded and left to die in agony. As a runner, he carried no rifle due to the weight. There was an Officers pistol hanging on a tent pole with no one around. Uncle Bland liberated that pistol and used it to put horses out of their misery whenever he passed. That put the mist in his eyes whenever he told that story.

While he was at headquarters one day Uncle Bland heard that there was a British Tank Group in the area. American volunteers were being sought to ride with the British tanks. Uncle Bland stood up and was assigned to a tank. He always said that riding wasn't a bad way to fight a war. The only problem was that the Brits carried a keg of rum and were constantly nipping at it. Uncle Bland was all for that until the Lieutenant decided to attack a German Machine Gun position upon a hill. Uncle Bland believing that discretion is the best part of valor opened the rear hatch and rolled out back down the hill. The drunken British Lieutenant died with his entire tank crew. Uncle Bland received a hearty "Well Done" for employing a magnificent strategic withdrawal.

Uncle Bland and Uncle John had never gotten along as children nor did they get along as adults. I never knew why they didn't like each other. I spent time with them both and still treasure my time with them. Uncle Bland was walking towards Nellysford on the old road below Winter Green House and Uncle John was walking the other way when they met. Uncle John pulled out his knife. Uncle Bland pulled out his pistol and shot Uncle John in the leg. Uncle John fell and rolled into a ditch. Not a word was said. Uncle Bland turned, walked back home and told Mammy Hughes that he shot John and left him in the ditch beside the road. Mammy Hughes made Bland hitch a wagon up and go get him while she took an ax and broke Bland's pistol. They just naturally didn't care for each other as my Father said.

When I was on my way to a duty station in Germany I stopped by to see Uncle Bland. When I told him I was going to Germany he said " Fine people those Germans I like them. Hated the French they piss on the street and eat

Horsemeat. Nastiest people I ever dealt. Don't have anything to do with the French."

One of Uncle Bland's big questions was why no one had thought about building a bridge from Virginia to France. In his opinion would have been real handy during the war and he would not have been seasick over there and back.

I saw him just before he passed away and he was still wondering about that bridge. I still miss him.

Aunt Sally Campbell

As a small child, I spent many hours sitting in the corner of her living room.

Aunt Sally Campbell was a well-known character who lived in Beech Grove. She was an older lady and one of those folks who either liked a person or not. There was no middle ground. In her world fools were not suffered lightly. She was a cousin of my fathers. Aunt Sally thought the world of my father and mother. They visited a great deal.

As a small child, I spent many hours sitting in the corner of her living room. When we arrived at her house the first thing she would do was make coffee. She had a special cup, saucer, and spoon for me. I was told to sit in the small chair and Aunt Sally would bring my coffee and a copy of her newspaper, the Baltimore Sun. She would always say be quiet, read the paper, and drink your coffee while the grown-ups talk. Remember, I couldn't read. The Baltimore Sun had very few pictures so I was kind of stuck for entertainment. Aunt Sally's opinion was, if you are a child and can't read you should listen. I learned to listen. They always talked about politics and news. I don't doubt that those conversations had a lot to do with forming my conservative views today.

Many years earlier Aunt Sally had married Mr. Campbell (I never knew his first name). They had a small farm between Montebello and Sherando. Apparently, neither one was easy to get along with. They were both very strong-willed. One morning, Mr. Campbell left the house to milk the cow. After about two hours Aunt Sally noticed that Mr. Campbell had not returned from milking. She went looking for him and found a bucket of milk hanging on a tree limb by the barn. She never heard from him again.

Aunt Sally lived in the Beech Grove and attended Christian Church; the rock church up there on the left. I never knew why the congregation sold the church to her but she lived there a few years. Before Moving to the church Aunt Sally had lived over in Sherando and served as housekeeper to her cousin Henry Hughes whose wife had passed away and he was bedridden.

Whenever we visited I always notice that Aunt Sally kept a pistol on the table by her reading chair. My father warned me every time to not touch it. He said she needed the pistol for protection because she was an old lady living alone and there were a lot of mean people around. One of my cousins, Billy Hughes used to walk by the church and he would yell at Aunt Sally trying to scare her. One day Aunt Sally stepped out on the top step with her pistol. She aimed it above his head and popped off about four rounds. After that Billy went by the church low crawling in the ditch on the other side of the road. Billy didn't give Aunt Sallie any problems after that. Of course, Billy's parents had no problems with what she had done and wondered if she missed on purpose.

The Beech Grove congregation finally got back together. They approached Aunt Sally with an offer for the church which she accepted. Landon Phillips sold her a plot of land at the corner of Route 151 and Beech Grove Road just passed his Drive-in Theater. She had a small house built but I don't think she was ever happy there. She complained that the traffic was too heavy and the noise bothered her.

This was all before the Wintergreen Resort was built. The last house on Beech Grove Road was a small frame house on the left almost at the current entrance to the Resort. Aunt Sally bought that house and lived out her life there. She was very happy up on that mountain. No traffic or noise to speak of.

Not long after she moved up there Merlin Campbell came into Small's store and reported that he had just come down from Beech Grove. As he came past Cub Creek Road he met a big old black Bear, his wife Mrs. Bear, and three little ones all carrying suitcases. Merlin stopped to offer a ride. Mr. Bear said "Mr. Campbell, just take us far as you can, we'll walk the rest of the way. We just can't live up on that mountain with that mean old woman."

When Aunt Sallie passed away she left my mother some of her things. Among the things were her pistol and her reading chair table. I still have her table by my chairs and had it with me in the service.

My mother did not like having the pistol around, so she gave it to someone.

Tom's Plan or Saving Tom's Butt

When I got there Tom was standing in the street with a bullhorn in his hand.

This event took place back in the late seventies while I was stationed at Coast Guard SAR-LE Station In Islamorada Florida as the Executive Petty Officer. The crew consisted of one Chief as Officer in Charge, myself as XPO and 28 men as crew. We had two 41ft SAR Boats and one 17ft outboard.

During those years the drug wars were the hottest topic for the Coast Guard. Drugs were being smuggled through the keys on a daily and nightly basis. Intelligence was a saleable commodity. No one could be trusted when enough money was on the table. Local Law Enforcement was especially iffy due to officers being on the take with kinfolk and childhood friends in the drug business. Our Chief was an alcoholic, spending most of his time in the local bars drinking on the smuggler's tab. They had no respect for the Chief or any Law Enforcement authority.

I received a call from Our District Office stating that two Custom Patrol Officers were being assigned to the Islamorada area. CG Station Islamorada was to cooperate and assist with any request. I will call them Tom and Jim. They were not undercover but they did not advertise themselves as customs agents either. After Tom and Jim arrived at Islamorada, arrests and seizures rose to make Islamorada the top Coast Guard Law Enforcement Unit in South Florida due to Intel supplied by those two.

At this time I was single and lived on the Station. My room opened into the Operations room so that I could be on call all the time. On this night at about 2 a.m. the watchstander knocked on my door and told me that there was a call for me on a non-official radio channel. Tom was on the radio and said he needed some help. He gave me an address on Key Largo and asked if I would draw a weapon and meet him down the street from this address. He asked if we could keep this between just the two of us for a while. Knowing Old Tom, I said OK but knew this could go any number of ways.

When I got there Tom was standing in the street with a bullhorn in his hand. He told me that he had some smugglers surrounded in a house down at the end of the street. When I inquired as to the rest of our force Tom admitted with my arrival we were now two strong. The house was on stilts on a cul de sac with a canal backing it up.

There was no one in sight as we approached the house. It was lit up and the dock lights were on. We could see burlap bales under the house and a few on the dock beside a large cigarette boat. Tom got behind a car in front and I went under the house behind the steps. Tom raised his bullhorn and announced that the U.S. Coast Guard and US Customs agents had the house surrounded and all occupants were to put down any weapons and exit down the steps with their hands in the air.

Five men, a woman, and a small child exited the house and walked down the steps. I searched and cuffed every one except the small child. One of the prisoners asked where the rest of our force was. I told him they were busy and couldn't be bothered by the likes of this group. Tom held them in place while I searched the house. I found six pistols and a couple of rifles with lots of ammo. There was still a lot of work left so I called the Station and had them send two men and a van to the address.

While waiting for the van I took inventory of the drugs and weapons. I then searched the house and boat while Tom stood watch on the prisoners. They seemed more upset at being surrounded by two guys than being arrested.

Tom and I seized 100 bales of drugs, a cigarette boat, a stilt house, and eight weapons. We arrested six armed smugglers. The child belonged to the woman. We were able to find the child's grandparents and they took custody.

We thought we were doing good until the command in Key West found out. They were not so happy until the District Admiral allowed as how he liked to see that kind of initiative. My Commander decided to be cool about the whole deal but stated that it would not happen again. The main thing he liked was that the Coast Guard and Customs were able to work well together He understood that sometimes things need to be done without advertising

A Marine Raised In The Blue Ridge Mountains

Billy Lee breezed through boot camp with no problems.

When I retired and moved back to the Rockfish Valley my neighbor was an old country Doctor That had practiced in this area his entire career. We spent many hours sitting and talking about the Valley and mountain folks who lived here. We both knew everybody and I was kin to most of them. He liked to hear my sea stories and I liked to hear his stories. He would always tell me to not repeat his stories using the real names and I have tried to keep to his instruction. This story is funny and also shows how tough these mountain boys are. They make good Marines because they are tough, honest, and loyal.

For this story's purpose, we will call the young man Billy Lee. Billy Lee had finished school and decided after a recruiter's relentless sales pitch to join the Marine Corps. The recruiter had told Billy Lee all about how wonderful the Marine Corps was. He has shown a picture of the Marine Corp Dress Uniform, and told about the adventurous life of a sea-going Marine guarding an Admirals hatch. Never was a thing said about the sand fleas, endless marches, poor food, godless drill sergeants, and warm beer.

Billy Lee breezed through boot camp with no problems. For a boy like Billy, Boot Camp was a walk in the park. He graduated and was given his 30 days leave to visit home.

The doctor was at his breakfast one morning when there was a knock on the door. It was Billy Lee's father and he told the Doctor that Billy Lee was sick and could not get out of bed. He asked the Doctor if he could come and see

Billy Lee. The Doctor followed Billy Lee's father up a long dirt and gravel road. The road ran out and they had to walk another mile to get to the log cabin where the family lived.

The father told the Doctor that Billy Lee was up in the attic where all the kids slept. The doctor climbed a pole ladder to get up in the attic. Billy Lee was laying under a pile of quilts on the floor. There was no heat and in fact, there was about a six-inch space between where the roof sloped down and met the first log. The wind was blowing snow flurries in through the spaces. The family acted as if they hadn't noticed the cold. They were some tough folks.

Billy Lee was very sick. He and a high temperature and was sweating heavily. He could barely talk. The Doctor examined him and explained that he had a bad case of pneumonia. He also told Billy Lee's father to pack Billy Lee's bag. The Doctor said to Billy Lee "I am going to take you to Charlottesville and put you on a bus back to South Carolina and when you get there give them this note." The note said "To whom it may concern. This boy has been weakened by the Marine Corps. He wasn't home more than a week and he contracted Pneumonia. He cannot live in these mountains in his condition. Hope you can recondition him back to where he was physically before you recruited him. Signed Doctor.............

This was in the late 1950s and early 1960s. Billy Lee was a fine Marine but never lived rough in mountains again.

Making Brandy Without A Permit At Old Winter Green

It was legal to make and sell brandy at that time if you had a permit.

Just after the century around 1901 or 02, there was an old Irishman named Gannaway who made apple brandy alongside Spruce Creek at Old Wintergreen. He was running four stills using Spruce Creek water and Rockfish Valley apples. It was said that some of the best apple brandy in Virginia was made there at Old Wintergreen by Old Man Gannaway. This was generally said by folks that had just drunk a jar.

It was legal to make and sell brandy at that time if you had a permit. Of course, old man Gannaway being the upstanding citizen that he was had a legal permit. He lived right on the property and was almost always available. He was legal.

Old Wintergreen was a busy place due to the grist mill, general store, post office, magistrate's office, and sawmill. On weekends there was a lot of drinking and general hell-raising. Old Man Gannaway got to a point where he needed help. He hired my Grandfather Gilbert Marshall who was around 20 years old at the time and newly married to help with the customer overflow. Old Man Gannaway thought he was the only one that needed a permit to sell brandy. He was wrong.

The County Sheriff stopped by and bought a jar from Gilbert. The Sheriff asked to see Gilbert's permit. Gilbert had no permit so he was arrested and taken to jail at Lovingston.

Tinsley Coleman was a cousin of Gilbert's wife Katherine. Tinsley was also a lawyer and a former Delegate to the State Legislature. When He heard about the arrest Tinsley told Katherine to not worry he would represent Gilbert. In Court Tinsley put on one of his best defenses casting Gilbert in the role of a poor defenseless young man employed by the unscrupulous still owner Old Man Gannaway who had not obtained the proper documentation for his poor employee Gilbert and was arrested by an overzealous Sheriff trying to make a name for himself by besmirching the name of one of the finest Virginia families.

Tinsley won the case and Gilbert was told to get a permit if he wanted to sell Brandy. The case was written into the Virginia legislature annual books and is there today.

Tinsley Coleman was a great lawyer. There were many cases where he distinguished himself. He got his Mother's Cook a not guilty verdict on a murder charge due to his mother's need for her cook. He also dumped a basket of rattlesnakes on the floor of the Virginia state legislature.

Tinsley Coleman was a great lawyer.

New York Harbor Patrol

About halfway through the Harlem River, there is a bar with a dock.

When my time was up at Coast Guard Loran Station Germany I was allowed to put in a request for my next duty station. My Commander, Lt. Hathaway, whom I did not get along with even a little bit called me to his office and told me that it would be to my advantage to request Governors Island, New York Harbor as that was what he had already requested for me. He was under the impression that I did not want to go to New York. Little did he know that was what I wanted. I complained and said it wasn't fair. That just assured me I would get to New York. Brer Rabbit could not have done a better job of acting. Please, Please don't throw me in the briar patch. That was how I got the New York Harbor Patrol. Spend all my time in a SAR Boat and wander around the harbor. No supervision, life was going to be good.

I reported aboard to Boatswain Mate Chief Torres. He welcomed me into his office, told me to take a seat, and commenced to give me the rundown on Sta. New York. He said that I probably would not see the Commanding Officer or Executive Officer any time soon because they spent all of their time nosing around the District Office sucking up to any senior officer they could find. Chief Torres was in charge, any problems or fixes went through him.   It sounded like my kind of Station.

I was checked out as a Coxswain (boat driver), assigned a boat with crew, and told to get underway patrolling the harbor. As part of the patrol, it was the boat crew's duty to stop boats and do a safety inspection, be on the lookout for and tow disabled boats, transport injured members of the boating public and any number of water-related mishaps. It was a great job.

A lot of humorous things happened. One evening at about 10 PM Chief Torres and I were in his office drinking coffee and swapping sea stories when the radio watchstander came over and told us that he had not received any radio checks for almost an hour from the duty boat. The coxswain of the duty boat that night was Billy Simpson from Texas. Chief Torres said, " He was supposed to circle Manhattan tonight, I hope he didn't stop on the Harlem River and send someone over in the Bronx side for fried chicken." Chief told me to round my crew up and go find Simpson.

About halfway through the Harlem River, there is a bar with a dock. When I got there Simpson's boat was tied up at the dock with no one aboard. The crew had tied the boat up, left their handheld radio on aboard, and went in the bar.

I called Chief Torres on the radio and told him what I had. He said to take the boat in tow and bring it back to the station. Don't go to the bar and alert Simpson. When I got back to the station Chief Torres was on the dock and laughing. He said the radio watchstander had received a call from Simpson stating that someone had stolen his boat. Simpson was told to take a taxi back to Governors Island but do not call any other law enforcement.

When Simpson got back Chief Torres told Simpson and me to go sit in his office. I asked Simpson why he had done something so stupid like that. He said he always stopped at that bar for a beer when he made that patrol. He just forgot his handheld radio this time. I allowed as to how it could happen to anybody.

When the Chief finally came into the office he never asked a question at all of Simpson. He just said that he thought the punishment should be handled by a Chief. He said that it takes to long to train a good man like Simpson. He told Simpson to go forth and sin no more or he would have someone kick his butt if it happened again. He followed with "Don't you know to carry your handheld radio at all times."

We were having coffee another time when the radio watchstander came in and said that Coxswain Gosnell had reported a collision with an 18 wheel trailer. Chief Torres asked the radio watchstander "Did you find out if he was drinking?". "Yes Sir," the radio watchstander said. Coxswain Gosnell said he collided with the trailer because it was underwater. The trailer had gone in the water off the Tappensee Bridge and no one had marked it.

Chief Torres never mentioned that fact in the reports. He just let it ride that a CG SAR boat had collided with an 18 wheeler and that the boat operator was one BM2 Gosnell.

Chief Torres to my knowledge never put anyone on report for misconduct or any violation. He took care of everything to do with the men himself. He said that was why God made Chief Boatswain Mates. Chief Torres opined that when you tell a man to strap an old rusty 40 foot SAR Boat to your ass and go out on that big blue water to save some hapless stranger then what more can you ask of him.

The Chief was right. I never have seen a Coxswain refuse to get underway, no matter the weather or the condition of the boat or crew.

The Coxswain motto will always be "YOU HAVE TO GO OUT BUT YOU DON'T HAVE TO COME BACK"

The Battle Of Fisher's Hill, September 21-22 1864

It happened that an artillery unit had just lost its officer from enemy fire. Aylett was told to take over the unit.

The Battle of Fisher's Hill was fought close to Strauseburg just south of Winchester in the Valley of Virginia. Three young men with ties to Winter Green took part in that battle. For the two that survived though they had never met before the war, their lives were forever connected.

Aylett Coleman was the youngest son of John J. Coleman, the owner of Winter Green Plantation. When the war started Aylett was a student at the University of Virginia. John J. wanted Aylett to study Law because the Coleman family tended to be of the litigious sort and he figured that having another lawyer in the family couldn't hurt. John J. had high hopes for Aylett to finish law school and return to Winter Green. His son Walker had finished Law School but he was the studious type and never showed any interest in the practice of law. Walker enjoyed the life of a rich planter's son and never considered working.

Three of Aylett's brothers were already in the Army. Sam served with the Stanton Artillery, Walker was with Pegram's Artillery and William was in a Calvary unit. Aylett decided that he could not stay in school while his brothers served their country. In the summer of 1864, John J. told Aylett to seek out General Imboden's headquarters and request a commission. General Imboden was a family friend and John J. thought that he would give Aylett a commission. John J. had written a letter to General

Imboden asking for a commission for Aylett and a place on the General's staff.

Aylett arrived at General Imboden's Headquarters on the 20th of Sept 1864. When General Imboden heard that John J. Coleman's son, Aylett, was at his headquarters seeking a commission the General told his aides to place Alyett where he was needed until a proper commissioning could be held.

It happened that an artillery unit had just lost its officer from enemy fire. Aylett was told to take over the unit. He was to keep close to the senior enlisted Sergeant and take advice from that Sergeant. Those gun crews knew their job and really didn't need an officer but it was traditional to have one anyway.

A short time after he joined the gun crew Aylett was hit in the chest by a rifle bullet. He was taken back to the medical tents but the doctors were unable to more than put a bandage on his chest. The next day he was taken by wagon to Woodstock and placed in a private home that had been turned into a hospital. Due to the primitive medical care that was available, Aylett passed just a few days after being hit.

The Battle of Fisher's Hill was lost but General Imboden took the time to ensure that Aylett's body was sent home to Winter Green where he lies in his grave by his father and brothers. Jacob Meeks was a poor farm boy born and grew up on the headwaters of Stoney Creek. He had only been to school enough to learn basic reading, writing, and arithmetic.

In those days every farm boy was proficient with a rifle. Being a good hunter sometimes made the difference between eating and starving. One day right after the war started Jacob's father sent him to the Winter Green grist mill with a couple of sacks of corn slung across a horse's back to be ground into cornmeal for the family's bread. There was a recruiting Sergeant from the Army there that day. He saw Jacob and asked him about his health and could he shoot. Jacob reached up on his horse and lifted both 50 lb sacks of corn off the horse with one hand. He then aimed his old flintlock rifle that had been handed down from his grandfather who had fought in the War Of 1812 at a bird about 150 yards away and knocked that bird off a tree limb.

The sergeant knew a potential fine soldier when he saw one. Jacob signed up right away and was given the time to go home say goodbye to his parents and be ready to move out the next morning Jacob's father was not happy but knew he could not hold Jacob back so he gave him his blessing. Told him to mind his betters and be a good boy.

Henry Judson Rittenhouse was born at Mt. Horeb which is not far from Winter Green. His family was better off than Jacobs Meeks family. They had a bigger farm on better land and owned a few slaves. This did not keep Henry from working the fields as a child. His father believed in work and the only time off was Sunday to attend the Baptist Church. Henry did learn to read, write, and some arithmetic. Mostly he learned to work.

When the war started Henry was recruited somewhat like Jacob. Henry didn't much like the Army. He was used to working hard and accomplishing something. The army worked hard and in Henry's eyes accomplished nothing.

Henry and Jacob only knew each other in passing. They had met a few times at Winter Green but didn't really know each other. They met again at Fisher's Hill when their units were put into the battle line beside each other. The night before the battle they met and talked of home and folks they both knew.

At dawn the Yankees attacked. The numbers were overwhelming. As the Southern Officers started to call retreat, Soldiers were left wounded and dying on the field. Jacob was running and firing with the rest when he recognized Henry. Jacob saw Henry fall and grabbed the soldier next to him and said "Hold my Rifle I got to go back and get Henry" With bullets whizzing around him, Jacob lifted Henry into what would be today called a Fireman's Carry and ran over a mile to an aid station. Henry was bleeding badly from his leg. Jacob took Henry into a surgeon's tent and told them to fix Henry and he would be back to check.

The field surgeon did what he could. Henry was put into a farm wagon with other wounded and sent over the mountain to Charlottesville where his leg was removed. After a while gangrene sit in and they had to remove more of his leg. He spent a long time coming to terms with the loss of his leg. After a while, he accepted his wound and went on to raise a family and had a successful life.

Jacob went on fighting and found himself near the end at Petersburg. He saw the end in sight and when the retreat started west he decided it was over and he would go home. One day as he was passing through Buckingham County he came across a man leading a horse with another slung over the horse's back. One of the men was Walker Coleman of Winter Green Plantation and the other was Warren Davis.

Walker had stolen an artillery horse to carry Warren. They had also quit the army and were going home. Warren was too sick to walk so they had stolen the horse.

After Henry was released from the Army Hospital at Charlottesville he returned home to his brother's farm. He lived with his brother for several years but he felt he was a burden on his brother. He heard that there was an opening for a farm manager's job at Glenthorne. Henry was able to secure that job at Glenthorne where he spent the rest of his life.

Jacob went back to live on his small farm on Stoney Creek. He and Henry became good friends and they helped each other whenever one or the other needed help.

The kind of bravery that Jacob showed on that day at Fisher's Hill, if displayed today would get a medal, promotion, and a TV Interview. Jacob got no recognition except Henry's everlasting gratitude.

Cousins

I have many cousins.

As a member of the Hughes family, I have many cousins. Of the many that stand out in my mind, are two of my favorites, Son Small and Doug Thompson. Now, some who know us would wonder how those two would be anybody's favorites. They were loud, sometimes vulgar, and other times downright mean. Most folks would tread lightly when they were around in order not to be their target of fun or ridicule. Those two boys stayed clear of each other due to their decades-old common dislike for each other. Keep in mind that they lived in the same neighborhood all their lives. The following are a couple of stories that they told about themselves.

Son's father was B.C. Small, who married my Aunt Anne. B.C. was a farmer and was elected Supervisor of the Rockfish District in Nelson County for about 25 years (It was rumored that Son's job was to give voters a ride to the polling places and provide whiskey on the way). When the counties first Extension Agent was hired he told B.C. that it would be a good idea to send samples of his soil to VPI and they would be able to advise him on what kind of crops to plant. B. C. had rented farmland all over the county so he gave a box of sample jars to Son and told him to go around to each parcel of rented land and get a sample. Son left early in the morning and got about five miles from home. He turned off onto an old dirt road and filled all the bottles from some dirt a farmer had plowed up. Son then spent the rest of the day sleeping in his pickup truck.

That evening Son got home just before dark with his box of full bottles of soil. B.C. was overjoyed that Son had done such a good job. The very day the box was shipped off to VPI for testing. About a month later B.C. received the soil report back from VPI. Son had been sweating this. He just knew that VPI would notice what had been done and write back that the soil was from one pile. The report that VPI sent back was about two inches thick and each sample jar had been thoroughly tested. No two jars tested the same and each gave differing crops that could be grown.

Son had always wanted a Lincoln Automobile and when he finally got to a place that he could buy one he went to a dealer in Richmond and got one. He told the dealer to put all the bells and whistles on it. He was so proud of that car that he thought that a trip was in order.   I don't think that Son had ever been out of the state of Virginia except when he was taking a load of apples to Georgia. He and his wife decided to drive out to Nashville. While in Nashville they went out to a fancy restaurant. The restaurant was one of those dark places with high prices. As Son was driving a Lincoln he ordered the most expensive meal. When the meal arrived Son dove right in and ate everything he saw. When the waiter came he asked Son if he enjoyed his meal. Son replied that it was a great meal except for the coconut cake which was dry and kind of chewy. The waiter informed Son that the coconut cake was a towel that most people used to wipe their hands.   Son's wife was not entertained.

After Son returned from his Nashville trip he got word that a good friend had passed away. He thought this would be a good opportunity to show off his new Lincoln Automobile. On the day of the funeral down at the Baptist Church Son got dressed up in a proper funeral suit and drove on down to the church. There was a big crowd. As good Baptist folk, the crowd was outside the Church milling around whispering to each other when Son drove up.

Everybody looked up when Son drove in and parked. He got out of the car, adjusted his coat, and pushed the car door shut. While walking away he heard a voice say, "THE DOOR IS AJAR". Son looked around trying to figure out who said that. He scratched his head and kept walking when again he heard the voice say "THE DOOR IS AJAR". A wag in the crowd said, "Hey Son, your car is talking to you".

As you can imagine Son was embarrassed to no end. He didn't stay for the funeral. He went straight home and called the dealer in Richmond to come and get this damn Lincoln and that he couldn't drive a car that talked and embarrassed him at a funeral.

Son lost some money on that deal but he got his pickup truck back (which did not talk) and he was happy.

Cousin Son was one of the most real people I have ever known. He was a character and could be as funny as any show business comedian. He was a good friend and I miss him.

Cousin Doug Thompson was another character who was entertaining and serious at the same time. He could walk into a room and make people nervous and afraid or he could make those same people laugh and have a good time. Doug was big and strong, he was no doubt the most fearless man in the valley. If Doug liked you, He would always be on your side, but don't cross him or you would live to regret it.

This incident happened back in the fifties. Doug stopped at a local store and as he parked his truck he saw a logging truck there with a horse tied on a flatbed with no sideboards. Doug went into the store and asked the driver to step outside. The man unwisely asked Doug how is it any of your business how I haul my horse. Doug replied with a fist to the guy's jaw. The man was taken to the hospital and had his jaw wired up. Needless to say, he never tried to haul his horse on a truck like that ever again and word got around that anyone harming an animal had better hope Doug Thompson did not hear of it.

Next door to Doug lived Old Man Bob Hughes who had been bedridden for a long time. The Doctor had told the family that Bob didn't have long to live, in fact, he would not last until daylight. The family and neighbors gathered to sit up with him until he was gone.

Doug noticed all these folks next door and he fixed coffee and food for the whole crowd. My mother was there that night and she said that the crowd was so surprised and they all couldn't believe that Doug had done such a nice thing.

Doug had a real serious side but he could also be kind and compassionate. I always liked to talk to him because I knew it was going to be a fun conversation. Whenever I drive through Nellysford I think about Doug Thompson and Son Small.

Alexander And Sally Hughes

John J. knew that his son Alexander needed a paying job now that he was getting married.

The Hughes and Napier families had been close for many years. The families had always gotten along well and had great respect for one another. It was no surprise that when Alexander and Sallie announced that they were getting married the families had no objections.

Alexander worked for his father John J. Hughes on his farm at Manley Springs up on Spruce Creek. He grew apples on the side of the mountain that goats would have trouble climbing. Alexander was the youngest son and he knew he was working for a place to live and eat. He received no salary because John J. believed that food and a place to sleep was enough payment.

John J. knew that his son Alexander needed a paying job now that he was getting married. He had heard that the Pharsalia Plantation in Massie's Mill was looking for an overseer. He sent Alexander over to Massie Mill where he was able through John J's influence to get the overseer's job.

The wedding was held at Manley Springs. The Napiers, being great hunters provided all the meat such as deer, bear, rabbit, and squirrels. The Hughes folk provided the Apple brandy and corn whiskey. From all accounts a grand time was had by all. Even though the Hughes and Napier family had known each other for so long there had not been any other weddings between the families. It was a very special occasion.

In those days it was a rare thing for a newly married couple to take a honeymoon trip. Alexander and Sallie rode horseback over the mountains through Mountain Field and Beech Grove. From there they rode over Cub Creek Road to the old Massie Grist Mill and Pharsalia. The trip took the whole day and Alexander was to begin work the next morning meeting the hands, walking the fields, and getting a hands-on feel for Pharsalia Plantation.

Alexander and Sallie spent the first few years of their marriage at Pharsalia. Alexander, being the youngest child of a large family had learned early how to be a good follower. Now as an Overseer He had to provide leadership to a group of field hands, some of whom had been slaves at Pharsalia. He proved himself as a natural leader by being first in the fields at sunup and last out at sundown. He was fair to the hands and made sure they were rewarded for good work.

Alexander saved enough while working at Pharsalia to buy 200 acres of land that his father had for sale on Spruce Creek. John j. Hughes was not one to give his son a break. When Alexander had the money John J. transferred the land to him.

The land had been cleared and an Apple Orchard planted. Alexander had a pretty good start but still had to build a home. They lived in a log cabin on the land just up from Sallie's brother Jim Napier. It was only one room with an attic. Sallie was happy because she was back close to her family on Spruce Creek. The new home was built about a quarter-mile from where it stands today over in the hollow where their youngest son Wirt lived later on. Sallie was very happy to have the new home. It was a typical

Virginia farmhouse. Two rooms over two with hallways and porches front and back.

Two years after they moved into their new home Sallie announced to Alexander that she was not satisfied with the location of their home. No doubt Alexander was very patient when he said "What the hell are you talking about and what do you want me to do about the location"? Sallie said that the new home would have to be moved over on the hill by the log cabin that they had lived in. She wanted to be close to her Sister-in-Law and brother Jim Napier. This was a distance of maybe a half-mile. After many heated discussions all of which Sallie won, Alexander finally gave in.

Alexander got a crew together and they took the new home completely apart plank by plank. The chimneys were taken apart brick by brick and the whole house was moved by horse-drawn wagon over to the hill where it stands today. Sallie was very happy until she realized there was no spring for water on that hill. This was no time for Alexander to say "I told you so".

Sallie was not happy about the water situation as she cooked for her family and the farmhands plus they had built quarters for a school teacher and the preacher. Alexander was on the hot seat again, he had to fix the water problem. His answer was, we have to dig a well. This news was announced to the sons, teacher, preacher, and farmhands.

The first fifteen feet wasn't bad as it was topsoil and red dirt. At fifteen feet they ran into rock, solid rock. With my Grand Ma Sallie on their butts, they had to keep going. The only thing to do was to start blasting. Holes had to be drilled with a rod and hammer then filled with black powder and a length of powder soaked cotton string was lit. The person had to then be pulled out of the well by a rope. My father, Tucker said it was probably the most fearsome thing he had ever done. They were to finally strike water at sixty-five feet. The well is still functional today. I pulled water out of that well in a bucket every day as a child. It was the best water I have ever had. I think it was so good due to the work to get it out of the ground.

Sallie was now happy. She had her home in the right place and plenty of water. She had four daughters to help cook and care for the home. There were also eight sons and several nephews to work in the orchards. The farm was very successful.

Straight down the hill from the new house, there was a small creek that flowed alongside the hill. The creek was the boundary marker between the Hughes land and the Harris land. Across the creek, there were about two flat acres before it went uphill. Now, there had been bad blood between the Hughes family and the Harris family for years. Alexander had the boys dig a new channel for the creek up against the Harris mountain. In that way, he gained two acres. The Harris fought it but the creek was the legal boundary whichever way it flowed.

Alexander opened a store at Winter Green down the road from his home that was also a Post Office that ran a Star Postal Route to the train station at Afton six days a week. My father Tucker rode horseback to Afton where he picked up the mail and delivered it to post offices on the way back to Winter Green. Alexander next bought the grist mill that ran off a raceway from Spruce Creek.

Sallie had to pretty much run the farm while Alexander took care of the Winter Green business. When Alexander was appointed Magistrate it meant a lot more organization and record keeping. He was responsible for registering births, deaths, wills, and land surveys. His lack of good record-keeping followed people for years especially when Social Security came in. There were very few who had their birthdays recorded right. Most went by what their parents told them but it was the record that Alexander made that counted. He was an old man by then so they had to accept it.

As Magistrate, Alexander most enjoyed settling disputes and disputes were something that Winter Green had plenty of. He would have the complainants meet at the front porch of his grist mill where he held court. There would always be a big crowd because Alexander's court was entertaining. Two neighbors were there one day and their argument was over a calf. One neighbor's bull had gotten to a neighbor's cow which got pregnant. They both claimed the calf. Alexander's decision was to wait until the calf was grown and either sell it and split the money or slaughter it and split the meat. Neither neighbor was satisfied. It was then that Alexander's son-in-law, Zach Hughes, got into the argument and said that Alexander was acting like old Kaiser Bill Over in Germany. Alexander couldn't take an insult like that so he reared back and kicked Zach in the jaw with his stove pipe boot. It broke Zach's jaw and he talked kind of funny the rest of his life. Alexander did not tolerate interference in his court.

Sallie had her hands full running the farm and orchard. She was also raising twelve children. Of course, Tucker was the oldest and had to take on the responsibility of working the farm under the supervision of his mother. The children were fairly well behaved as I understand it. There were many small flare-ups between the boys but there was so much work they didn't have time to fight but so much. Some fighting between brothers is expected and in some ways, healthy. Of course, farm work came first.

During World War 1 tragedy struck the family. Most of the boys had to go off to war. Bland and Jack were sent to the battlefields of France. Jack was gassed during the war and returned a broken man. He was never able to work and after a few years was sent to the veteran's hospital in Tennessee where he passed away. Bland on the other hand talked as if the war was the high light of his life. He talked to me of the great times he had and the sights he had seen. Too Bland, it was as if the war was made for his enjoyment. I spent many happy hours on his porch listening to his stories.

I am proud to be the grandson of Alexander and Sallie. I was the youngest Grandson born a few years after they had passed away. All of my Uncles and Aunts told me stories of their childhood and growing up on Spruce Creek above Winter Green. It has always been a disappointment that I never knew them.

Tucker C. Hughes

One of the duties of Post Master at Winter Green was that someone had to ride horseback to the Afton train station, pick up the mail and deliver it to Avon, Greenfield, Nellysford, and Winter Green.

Tuck was born in 1884 in a log cabin on Reids Creek close to where it runs under Route 151 today. He was the first of twelve children born to Alec and Sallie Hughes. Tuck was lucky to be the firstborn. Of course, I am sure he didn't see it that way. He was put in a position of responsibility for the rest of the children as they were born. As his mother and father were busy running the farm and Winter Green business. Tuck had not only to work on the farm, he had to help his mother care for the children. The four girls gave very little problem. In Tuck's opinion, the girls were all little ladies. On the other hand, the boys were all little hellions whose main function was to make his life miserable. Being the oldest It was Tuck's duty to watch over and take care of the young ones. They used Tuck as a sounding board even after becoming adults and having their own children.

When Tuck's father Alec was working as overseer at Pharsalia, Tuck was in the tobacco fields working alongside the hands. He planted, worked, wormed, cut, and helped cure the tobacco in smokehouses. After smoke curing the tobacco had to be packed into hogsheads for shipment to Lynchburg. Raising tobacco was a hard backbreaking job and it involved everyone on the plantation. Even women and children had to worm the tobacco because their hands were tender and did not bruise the tobacco leaves as they removed the worms.

Alec finally had saved enough to buy two hundred acres from his father John J. on Spruce Creek. When the family moved to their new land Tuck was an experienced field worker. At the new home, Tuck had a new experience. His Mother's brother Jim Napier had built a small schoolhouse just down the hill from Tuck's new home. He was sent to school to learn to read, write, and do arithmetic. Of the subjects taught reading was the only one that Tuck thought was worthwhile. It must have been something in their nature because all the Hughes Family were readers. It was often said if you want to keep a Hughes quiet put a book in his hands.

Alec made sure his kids all had plenty of work to keep them busy. An apple orchard was a year-round job as much so as tobacco had been. The orchards were planted on hillsides because flat land was used to grow tobacco, corn, and other field crops. The hillsides had to be cleared of trees and brushes. After planting the grafting had to be done. Grafting was when cuttings from the type of apples you wanted to grow were attached to a rootstock. This was something of an art, and only experienced hands were allowed to do it. It took three to five years to get a crop from a new orchard. Meanwhile, the mature orchard had to be pruned, sprayed and the fruit picked and packed for shipping. Any downtime was used for making and stamping barrels even though the cooper made the barrels, there was a great deal of work today for all hands.

Alec spent most of his time at Winter Green running the mill, the store, and the post office. A great deal of Alec's time was taken up with his duties as Magistrate and Post Master. One of the duties of Post Master at Winter Green was that someone had to ride horseback to the Afton train station, pick up the mail and deliver it to Avon, Greenfield,

Nellysford, and Winter Green. He then spent the rest of the day working on the farm.

It was not all work for Tuck. On weekends there was always a dance or party somewhere and there you would find Tuck. Tuck's Uncle Henry Hughes lived over across the mountain in Sherando. On Saturday morning he would saddle one of the horses and ride over to Sherando to attend one of the many home dances held every Saturday night. It was a long ride. He rode over to Stoney Creek, then to the top and through a pass between two rocks that he said you could only ride a skinny horse through. What made the trip so long was that Tuck would stop and talk at every house picking up and passing on gossip. Tuck was quite popular. Uncle Henry was a widower and Tuck was about the only company he had. Most of Sunday was spent talking to Uncle Henry. Then it was back across the mountain to Spruce Creek for another full week of work on the farm.

Tuck didn't spend every weekend at Sherando. There were social occasions all around the Southern Rockfish Valley. Folks were having dances and get-togethers in their homes every weekend. Tuck had four sisters and being the oldest he had to chaperone whenever they wanted to attend a dance. It proved to be a good thing because the boys were not always gentlemen.

One of the sisters wanted to go to a dance on Stoney Creek. There was a boy there named Singleton Harris, whose family had been feuding with the Hughes family for years. Singleton had of course been drinking heavily as any Harris is wont to do. As Tuck's sister passed, Singleton stuck his foot out and tripped her. Tuck saw it happen and invited Singleton outside to settle the matter. Tuck's mistake was walking in front of Singleton. Singleton picked up a stick of wood and when Tuck turned Singleton hit him in the eye with the stick. Tuck lost sight in that eye for the rest of his life.

The feud between the Hughes and Harris Families escalated after that. Nobody was killed but there were many an instant where shots were exchanged. Singleton was found lying in a ditch drunk with a broken leg. A few years later he was sent to the penitentiary for theft. His still and all his whiskey was missing after a night of drinking with some Hughes relatives. Singleton woke up laying by the fire where his still had been. Old Singleton had bad luck the rest of his life after attacking Tuck in a cowardly manner.

Singleton wasn't the only Harris that had bad luck. Kaolian Harris, one of Singleton's brothers started having bad headaches late in life and his sister took him over to UVA. After being examined the Doctor came in and told Kaolian that he was going to have to operate because when they took X-rays they found a lot of black spots all over his head and back. Kaolian told the doctor he didn't think an operation would be necessary because the spots were lead birdshot where one of those damn Hughes brothers had shot him 30 years ago.

In 1954 Grover Harris was killed when he fell into the water box while working off a ladder above his grist mill wheel at Winter Green. Tuck used to say that the only Harris that was any account was old man John Wills Harris who had bought Winter Green in 1900 when the Coleman descendant was forced to sell. John Wills Harris had been a soldier of the Confederacy but his sons were lazy drunks who did nothing but drink and argue with everybody. They let the Winter Green home fall apart and it is almost gone today.

Tuck and his brothers were well-liked by everyone in the Winter Green Neighborhood. They were welcome wherever they went because they brought good cheer and funny stories. A story they still repeat today that Tuck told over at Jik Napiers house is still repeated today. It went like this. Every Sunday the Davis and Napier family had all their family come for Sunday dinner. My mother was a cousin so we were there. Tuck came late and when he came through the door he had this long sad look on his face. Roy Napier asked Tuck what was the matter cause Tuck was always smiling and in a good mood. He said that he had some bad news. It seems that poor old Margie Campbell was taken to the UVA Hospital last night. Well, everybody was sitting around wondering what was the matter with poor Margie who was a rather large lady, a good bit bigger than her husband, Henry. Tuck said that it seems that Henry and Margie were getting a bit frisky last night and Margie had got her big toe caught in her earring. That story broke the crowd up and everybody got a good laugh but Margie never forgave him and would do whatever she could to irritate him.

Tuck loved to pull jokes on folks. I remember that tourist would drive up Spruce Creek Road and see Tuck working. They would stop and ask if they could get to The Blue Ridge Parkway on this road. Tuck would tell those folks that of course you can drive up Spruce Creek Road and get to the Parkway. No Problem. It gets kind of narrow in places but you can make it. He would go on telling them what a great drive they were in for and how Spruce Creek Road wound around the most beautiful mountain country in

Virginia. He spun a wonderful tale of what they were in for. Of course, you could not drive to the Parkway on Spruce Road. You could get stuck up there and have to walk back down to Nellysford to get help. Tuck could not be found. He was over at Roy Napier's laughing about what he had done to a stranger.

Tuck's own family didn't escape his humor. His Uncle Jim and Aunt Missouri was his closet neighbor. The Napiers were great hunters. Tuck told the story that one time his Aunt Missouri got up in the middle of the night, walked out in the yard, stuck her nose in the air, and sniffed. She could smell a bear but didn't want to wake the boys up to go and get him. Aunt Missouri followed the smell about two miles up in the mountains and found that bear up a tree. She took her petty coat off and wrapped it around the tree causing the bear to be afraid to come down. She came back home, went back to bed, and when she got the next morning she sent one of the boys to get the bear and bring him home. Tuck told that story many times and always declared it was the truth.

Tuck was 62 years old and my mother was 44 when I was born. It was like having parents and grandparents. I had a wonderful childhood. In the Hughes tradition, I called my parents Pappy and Mammy. As a child, I thought Pappy knew everything. He did know a lot and if he didn't know he could give a really good answer. He was a reader and was seldom seen without a book or newspaper in his hand. He taught me things like when to plant peas and potatoes (St. Patricks' Day), how to follow a honey bee to its hive, and how to skin a squirrel. He gave me so much knowledge that I have never used but it is stored away in my head.

Tuck did not go to church but he was probably one of the best Christians in the neighborhood. He thought that preaching was not a job but a calling. If a preacher didn't have a job Tuck didn't think much of him. I only remember two preacher's he liked one was Rev. Farris, who was a carpenter like Jesus, and Riley Fitzgerald, who was a farmer. When Tuck was 75 years old Rev. Ferris talked to him about being baptized. Tuck allowed as how it couldn't hurt, so he was Baptized. Tuck practiced his faith privately and thought that his salvation was between him and the Lord.

Tuck practiced his religion quietly but put his political thoughts out there. He did not care for the Democrats at all. I remember a visitor was talking to Tuck and asked why he was so against Democrats. Tuck explained that Franklin Roosevelt stole all the land up on the mountain to build the Skyline Drive and drove all the people down to the valley. Tuck explained that it had taken years to get all the Shifflets and others confined up on the mountain and Roosevelt comes along and turns them loose back in the valley where they are breeding like rabbits. Tuck did not like Kennedy because his middle name was Fitzgerald. Tuck was of the opinion that no good could come of it. Maybe his reasoning was a bit off but he was right about no good could come of the Democrats.

Tuck passed away in 1964 and I joined the Navy in 1965. I spent 20 years in the service between the Navy and Coast Guard. In those 20 years, a good bit of it was at sea and aboard Search and Rescue boats. In all the bad weather and dealing with armed smugglers I always thought that Tuck was looking over my shoulder. The older I get the more I miss him and I always have the hope that he will be waiting at the Golden Gate for me.

The Brothers Hughes, William And Moses

William served alongside Thomas Jefferson as a Vestryman for St. Anne's parish.

I was about 12 years old on a cold, snowy, winter day. It was too cold to work outside and everyone was stuck indoors. I asked my father Tucker, whom I called Pappy why the two Hughes families here in Nelson County did not claim kinship. Pappy said that as there was nothing else to do he would explain what happened many years ago far beyond anyone living would remember. The story had been passed to him by his father Alec Hughes but he didn't think anyone else remembers. Most thought they were not kin and didn't care anyway.

The Rockfish Hughes families are descendants of William Hughes and the Massie's Mill Hughes Families are descendants of William's younger brother Moses.

Thomas Hughes and his wife Mary were the parents of William and Moses. William was born in 1743 and Moses was born in 1745 at the Hughes Plantation along the Fluvanna River in Goochland County. Thomas eventually bought another Plantation in Buckingham County near Scottsville. The brothers lived with Thomas and their mother in Buckingham until the end of the War of Independence.

The Hughes Plantation was very successful with the brothers overseeing the slaves and working alongside them in the fields. Neither one could be accused of laziness. After a few years, Thomas Hughes sold his Buckingham Property and moved to Scottsville in Albemarle County. The land in Buckingham had been worn out from Tobacco because they did not practice crop rotation. Tobacco was the main cash crop and overplanted due to it's value to the Colony. Their thought was that there is plenty of lands and we can always move West.

During the War for Independence, the Hughes Family raised crops for use by the American Army such as corn, oats, hay, potatoes, and beef. They made very little money during the War but were considered Patriots and are included in the Daughter of the American Revolution (DAR) which is quite an honor.

Thomas Passed away in 1779. His son William was the eldest, therefore, was named Executor of his father's Will. Thomas, in accordance with the customs of the time, left all his land and half his money to William. The rest of his estate went to the three younger brothers and sisters.

There was, of course, an argument over the Will. Because Moses believed that as he had put time and work on the farm he should inherit half, bedamned, to custom. No one had sympathy for Moses so he moved to Amherst County and bought mountain land west of Massie's Mill. It was poor land and cheap at the time. About the only thing, it was good for at was running hogs in the early Spring and Summer for the Fall Slaughter.

Moses never got over the argument. His modern descendants finally forgot what the quarrel was about but they knew they were not to ever claim kin with the other Hughes Family. Even now 200 years later some of Moses' descendants don't claim kin with William's descendants even though the connection has been proven by DNA. Just goes to show that the Hughes family never forgives or forgets a perceived slight.

William stayed in Scottsville on the land that he inherited. He had rich flat bottomland that was good for growing tobacco, corn, oats, and wheat. William had learned the method of crop rotation and used this method on his plantation. His crops were always good quality and he very became wealthy.

William served alongside Thomas Jefferson as a Vestryman for St. Anne's parish. It was said that Jefferson attended church very seldom. The duties could not have been great. William also served as Magistrate until he was elected Sheriff of Albemarle in 1797

In 1813 William passed away leaving the greater part of his Estate to his son John Jackson Hughes. John Jackson Hughes was named after Andrew Jackson of Tenn. This was before he was the Hero of the Battle of New Orleans.

John Jackson Hughes had spent his entire life working on his father's plantation just to the west of Scottsville. The land around Scottsville eventually wore out from overuse by raising tobacco. John realized that if he was to continue as a farmer he must move and change crops. He moved to the Woods Mill area in the late 1840s.

During the 1860s, apples became a popular crop in Virginia due to Queen Victoria's fondness for the Albemarle Pippin. The railroad lines through Afton and Rockfish made shipping long distance no longer a problem.

John Jackson went looking for land to plant an apple orchard. The new ground on a mountain slope was deemed the best for apples. He found good land in the Southern Rockfish Valley on the upper reaches of Spruce Creek at Manley Springs. The family moved there and planted an orchard.

After the family was settled, John Jackson decided to contact his cousins (The children of his Uncle Moses who lived over the mountain around Massie's Mill). He wanted to find out if they still held a grudge over their Grandfather William's will. They still held a grudge and would not even discuss a meeting to make up and act as a family.

John Jackson returned to Manley Springs, gathered his family around, and declared that they were no longer kin to the Moses Hughes family due to their inability to accept a legal Will. Until the advent of DNA, John Jackson's declaration has held. Once the DNA tests were done the families have gradually, with reluctance accepted that they are indeed kin.

Some of the older folks are a bit skeptical, but skepticism is a family trait for every Hughes I have ever met.

Hayward L. Dameron

(USMC, USN Ret. 1894-1920)

In 1894 Hayward ran away from home intending to go to Norfolk and join the Navy.

I recently wrote a story about my Uncle Russell Marshall who ran away from home and joined the Marine Corps at the age of 14. Uncle Russ and the Marine Corps did not work out well. It was not at all what Uncle Russ thought it was so he admitted he was only 14 and was sent home.

My Aunt Sally's husband Hayward Dameron was entirely different. Hayward was born in Nelson County in 1880 and for the first fourteen years of his life, he worked on his father's farm from daylight to dark every day except Sunday. He received about 4 years of school learning to read and write fairly well. The year he turned fourteen Hayward decided that he was grown up enough to be on his own.

In 1894 Hayward ran away from home intending to go to Norfolk and join the Navy. He walked and caught wagon rides to Norfolk. Some days he would go by a farm and ask for work just to be fed as he had no money. Farmers were always needing help so finding work for a meal was easy.

When Hayward reached Norfolk he had no idea how to join the Navy. There was a man in uniform standing in front of a building. Hayward stopped and asked the man where he might be able to join the Navy. The man asked Hayward how old he was. When Hayward replied that he was seventeen the man said follow me. Hayward, who was used to do what he was told followed the man.

In 1894 there was no formal recruiting office for the Marine Corps. Recruits were usually brought in by other Marines. There was no age checks or physicals. If you looked like a healthy man that was all it took. Uniform issue and training was done at the closest base. After the preliminaries, Hayward was assigned to a ship getting underway for Manila in the Philippines to be assigned to a ship's marine complement in the Asiatic Fleet.

For a 14-year-old kid, Hayward turned out to be a great Marine. He followed orders to the letter, wore a sharp uniform, and was an expert rifleman. The duties for a marine aboard a naval ship were fairly easy, He mainly did cleaning details and guarding the ship's officers.

This was the time of the Boxer rebellion in China when the Chinese wanted all Westerners and Japanese out of China. While Hayward's ship was at Taku the American Minister requested a Marine detail be provided to the American Legation in Peking. All foreign legations were under attack constantly. Hayward distinguished himself as an outstanding Marine. Hayward's unit was assigned to march into North China when it was decided to attack the rebellion with the intent of ending the conflict and restoring trade and peace in China.

In 1902 Hayward had eight years in the Marine Corps. In those days rank was slow and Hayward had made Corporal. His life was pretty good at that rank but he had been in battle the entire time he had been in China and he was getting tired. At this time his unit was assigned to the USS Brooklyn ACR 3 serving in the Asiatic Fleet.

Hayward decided that he would take his Marine Corps discharge and reenlist into the Navy as part of the USS Brooklyn's crew. His request was granted and in 1902 he was enlisted as a Seaman 1st Class into the US Navy and assigned to the Deck Division. The Navy had been Hayward's choice back in1894 when he had been hoodwinked by a Marine.

The Brooklyn was soon after detached from the Asiatic Fleet and sent to New York with a stop at Havana Cuba. Hayward liked the Navy and it's a more laidback way of life compared to the Marine Corps. He was always a hard worker and knew how to follow orders. It didn't take long for him to come to the attention of the Deck Chief Boatswain Mate who recommended him to be promoted to Petty Officer.

In 1905 the Brooklyn was ordered to proceed to Cherbourg, France where she would embark the body of John Paul Jones and proceed to the United States Naval Academy at Annapolis, Maryland for re-interment. While in Cherbourg, France Hayward was given the honor of being chosen as a Sideboy for John Paul Jones when his body was piped aboard. Being chosen to act as Sideboy is an honor that few receive. It goes to the most squared away sailors aboard the ship chosen by the Chief BoatswainMate.

Hayward remained aboard the Brooklyn his entire Navy career. During World War 1 she carried troops to France and escorted supply convoys to England and France. She was under constant threat of attack from German submarines and the German Surface Fleet.

Hayward spent his entire Naval Career aboard the USS Brooklyn. He retired as a Chief Boatswainsmate in 1920 after serving 26 years in the US Marine Corps and the US Navy. During those years travel for a military person to visit home was almost impossible. Hayward had not been home since he left at the age of fourteen.

My Aunt Sally Marshall was twenty years old that summer when Hayward returned home. She of course had never met him nor barely heard of him. In those days young folks worked hard on the farm all week but come Saturday night there would be a dance held in someone's home. On the Saturday night that Hayward met Aunt Sally the dance was held at Uncle Pal and Aunt Hettie Thompson's home on Stoney Creek. When Aunt Sally saw Hayward she asked him to dance right away. They danced every dance that night and when the group who lived on Spruce Creek left Hayward walked Sally all the way home holding her hand.

When Hayward heard there was a piece of land for sale on Spruce Creek beside Aunt Sally's father he bought it and asked Aunt Sally to marry him. She accepted and his traveling days ended right there. They lived on that small farm raising a family of two girls until Aunt Sally passed away in 1965.

Hayward had been born in 1880 and my father Tucker Hughes had been born in 1884 and when Hayward returned they became good friends. Tucker married Aunt Sally's sister Doris Marshall.

When I was a child I would sit and listen to them tell tales. Hayward didn't talk a lot about the wars because I think he didn't believe children should hear it. He did talk of the times aboard ship and Liberty towns. I loved to hear him talk about his tattoos and how they were applied. He said that a Chinaman with sharp bamboo sticks punched the holes in his skin and rubbed the ink in with his fingers. No antiseptic was used. Those were stories that made a little boy want to be a sailor.

I always thought that Uncle Hayward was the most interesting person I have ever met to this day. He had an impact on me that decided that I would join the Navy. The best decision I could have made.

A Family At Montebello

One thing they had plenty of was chestnut trees.

Rufus Fitzgerald was 17 years old towards the end of the War of Northern Aggression. He had lived his whole life at Montebello high up on the mountain towards the Southwestern part of Nelson County. Today the Blue Ridge Parkway goes right by it. Rufus had married and he lived with his wife Lucy Ann in a small log cabin built by their parents and neighbors, nestled up against a steep mountainside.

Life was hard at Montebello back then and truth be known hasn't changed much. Rufus had been given a few acres where he raised corn for bread and vegetables. For their meat, he kept a couple of hogs and hunted. Wild game was abundant in those high mountains such as bears deer, squirrels, and rabbits. They ate well up there but there was no money for clothes, coffee, sugar, flour or gun powder, and lead.

One thing they had plenty of was chestnut trees. The mountains were covered with them and folks living up there depended on them for the little cash earned from them. In the fall when chestnuts fell, hogs were turned loose to fatten up on the chestnuts that covered the ground. Some of the meat was cured and sold in Waynesboro. Chestnuts were also picked up and hauled down to Waynesboro to be shipped up north to the cities like Washington, Baltimore, and New York. Chestnut trees were also stripped of bark and sold to the leather tannery in Waynesboro.

Rufus and his neighbors knew there was a war going on but they figured that as they lived up at Montebello they were not involved. They just went along doing as they had always done. There were no newspapers and nobody could read anyway. All they knew was the little they heard, taking goods to Waynesboro and that wasn't much because once their business was done, they would leave straight back to Montebello to avoid all the thieves in Waynesboro.

The family had about run out of all of their store-bought goods and Rufus needed to take a load of tanbark to sell in Waynesboro and stock up. As Rufus was going through town to the tannery, he noticed a lot of soldiers milling about town drinking and generally raising hell. Rufus just wanted to get back on the mountain but he had one little stop to make.

Well, as Rufus was a Fitzgerald and like every Fitzgerald that ever walked on his hind feet, Rufus liked a little taste of Irish whiskey or whatever had alcohol in it. On his way out of town, he decided to stop at the hotel out by the railroad depot and have a little dram.

When Rufus got to the hotel a squad of Confederate Soldiers was hanging around outside on the porch. When Rufus walked up on the porch a soldier got up and said to Rufus "Hello there old son, would you care for a wee drink on the Confederate Army. Today is Generals Lee's birthday and our Captains is buying drinks at the bar to celebrate". Rufus, not being a man of the world and a bit naïve thought, this was nice of the captain. Rufus had a couple of shots of the most dreadful, vile-tasting rotgut he had ever had. Rufus was looking kind of sick so the soldiers took his arm and led him out the back door. There was a wagon full of passed-out young men sitting there and the soldiers hit Rufus on the back of the head and tossed him in.

Rufus woke up the next morning lying in a field surrounded by about 20 other men. A soldier walked over and started kicking everybody awake. He said "Ya'all are in the Confederate army now. Get over to the cook tent and get a piece of hardtack and salt meat. After you finish that, we will issue every man a musket, powder, and balls. Do this quickly we are moving out. There's a battle to be fought up the valley."

Rufus got the soldier's attention and says "I ain't in the army. I come down to sell my tanbark. Now my money is missing and you tell me I am in the army. I need to get home to my family." The soldier said "You people are in the Army now and any man caught running will be shot down like the cowardly dog he is. Now eat up and get your musket."

After marching for a few days Rufus and his fellow soldiers caught up with the army as they were going into battle. Rufus was put in a line of soldiers and told to advance. He didn't know what advance meant so he just did what everybody else did. He walked forward and got off a few shots.

Over there in the Shenandoah Valley, there are a lot of limestone caves. Some are just holes in the ground and if you are not careful you can easily fall in one. You might fall 10 feet or a hundred feet. Back then they were not marked. As Rufus was advancing, he just disappeared. Nobody noticed because of all the shootings.

After a few hours, Rufus finally came awake and looked up. He was about ten feet down in the hole. It was easy to climb out and he looked around. There were dead bodies everywhere and Rufus was frightened out of his mind. The Army was gone. Rufus figured he was left for dead so he was on his own. Rufus was a long way from home but he was a mountain boy and knew his directions. Looking east he saw the mountains and knew all he had to do was walk south.

Rufus remembered what the soldier said about anybody running would be shot so he started home traveling mostly at night. He took vegetables from people's gardens, stole chickens, and one time snuck up to a house and took a pie out of the kitchen window that had been left to cool.

What with all the hiding and traveling at night it took about two weeks for Rufus to get back to Montebello. Lucy thought he had been killed and she was overjoyed that he was able to get back home. Rufus was afraid that somebody would come looking for him. He didn't know that nobody missed him. He was not listed on the company books. He had just been impressed into the army as cannon fodder. If anyone thought of him at all they just thought he was killed. He wasn't with the army long enough to be just a number.

All Rufus knew was that a soldier could be shot for running. The back wall of their cabin backed against the side of the mountain. Rufus cut a hole in the back of the cabin and dug out a cave into the side of the mountain and hung a quilt over the hole. He told Lucy to not tell anyone he was back. He would go out at night to hunt and work the crops on moonlit nights. During the day he stayed in the cave.

Some of the family found out and tried to get him to come out of the cave and live normally. But Rufus was so traumatized he just could not do it. He lived like that till he died in the 1920s.

After a few years, Lucy Ann gave birth to a child who was given the name Riley. As Riley grew, he realized that his daddy Rufus was not normal. He was sure that the soldiers would come and take him back to the war. The few strangers that wandered to Montebello put Rufus in a bad mental state that took weeks to get over. This all placed a terrible strain on Lucy Ann and she dealt with it through the small church at Montebello. Her religion was her life.

Lucy Ann wanted to be sure that Riley would not grow up like Rufus so she made him attend church with her every Sunday. Neither Rufus nor Lucy Ann could read nor write but she made Riley attend the one-room log school built by the community and taught by an old preacher named Rev. Watson who had been a circuit preacher that rode horseback through the mountains preaching the gospel to whoever he found in every community he rode through. Rev. Watson was getting on up in age and he was looking for someone to take his place in watching over his flock of sinners in the mountains.

It was a good thing that Riley wasn't a lazy boy because he was out every night with his daddy hunting or working the farm and going to school during the day and church on Sunday. It was a hard life for Riley as a boy and young man. All of Montebello knew that Rufus was not right in the head so they could forgive him that and at the same time admire Riley for taking care of the family at a young age

Well, you got to remember that even though Riley, as a young person was so well thought of, a hard worker, and very religious he was still a Fitzgerald at heart. Riley and his daddy had cut an oxcart load of tanbark and due to Rufus and his fears of the outside world, it was up to Riley to take a load of tanbark to Waynesboro.

Riley got the load to the tannery, unloaded it, and got his money. As he was headed back out of town on the way to Montebello, he had to pass the very same hotel where Rufus had met his Waterloo. Riley decided to stop and have a little dram and due to him being a Fitzgerald one was not enough. Riley woke up with the sun in his eyes. He was lying in a ditch with nothing but his britches and galoshes to hold them up. His ox, oxcart, money, shoes, and shirt were gone. The only thing that was missing was the army that got his daddy.

Riley's mama had pushed him into religion all his life and he had been taught a lot of religion by the Rev. Watson. When he got home Riley told his mama what had happened and asked her to go with him to see Rev. Watson.

Riley and his mama met with Rev. Watson in his cabin. Riley told Rev. Watson what had happened. He asked Rev. Watson to pray with him. He wanted the Lord to forgive him and put him on a path of righteousness. Rev. Watson told him that the Lord would forgive him but he had to find his path by obeying the word of the Lord and seeking his forgiveness and righteousness. The Fitzgerald family tries hard to follow the Lord and obey his word but they have a weakness for the devil alcohol. You, Riley, will always bear that burden.

Rev. Watson advised Riley to go home and get a good night's sleep and come back to his cabin the next day. Rev. Watson had been keeping an eye on Riley for some time and he had marked him to take over his circuit ride through the mountains preaching to the mountain people. It was a hardscrabble way to love cause you have no wife and kids due to the constant travel. The only compensation was a bed or floor pallet in someone's cabin. You might get a sack of turnips or a bottle of homemade spirits. Riley took the circuit and never looked back. It was the perfect life for him. He knew he was doing the Lord's work.

GRIST MILLS ON SPRUCE CREEK
THE FIRST

The first grist mill on Spruce Creek was built by Hawes Coleman in the early 1800s. It was built up the creek from where Route 151 goes over the bridge. The mill was built of a rock first floor and two floors of brick made on the property. The mill pond was about a half mile upstream from the mill made by digging out a large pond in Spruce Creek. There was a high bank above the creek and the raceway was dug into the side of that bank leading downstream to the mill. The raceway was dug with a slightly slanted elevation the entire half mile to a wooden trough to pour water over the wheel. These works can still be seen today. The tail race had a canal dug to take the water back into Spruce Creek.

At the time this mill was built it was the only mill in the southern part of Rockfish Valley. Farmers from all over came there to have their corn ground for bread and livestock feed. It was also a social hub as mills were in those days. Farmers gathered there on Saturdays to drink, gossip, drink, and fight. They also had their corn ground.

During the War of Northern Aggression when the godless Yankees started their War against the farmers over in the Shenandoah Valley, they destroyed everything they could having to do with food production. Crops were destroyed, barns burned, animals killed, and females of all ages were raped and beaten. It was a time that showed what the Yankees really were. Foreign scum of the earth that the Yankees had drafted into their Army.

The Yankees tended to spill over into the eastern Blue Ridge Valleys. As they rode south from Afton they left a path of destruction and thievery behind them. They rode up to the Grist mill on Spruce Creek and were most impressed.

Most mills of that time were jury rigs built of green lumber and all working parts except the grinding stones were wood. Not so with the Wintergreen mill. It was stone, brick, and metal.

The Yankee Captain looked at this marvel of engineering and said "Well boys this will take a little more than fire to destroy. Anybody got any ideas." The junior officers stood about saying nothing. Finally, an old Sergeant speaks up and says "It will take about 5 kegs of powder to take her down." The Captain says " Well Sergeant, You just volunteered to take some men and go back to Afton and bring back 5 Kegs of gunpowder. Don't forget that there are people in this valley that can and will shoot you from a great distance so do be very careful and don't tarry."

The Old Sergeant and his boys got kind of thirsty on the way back from Afton and stopped at an old farmer's house down by Greenfield. The old farmer happened to have some homemade whiskey that he was more than happy to share with the Yankee soldiers. The soldiers hadn't had a drink for some time and they soon passed out. When they woke up the farmer and his boys were gone. Each keg had been opened and half the powder was removed. That left them with five kegs but only two and one-half kegs of powder. The Old Sergeant had been around a long time and knew the score. He filled up the half-empty kegs with sand.

Back at the mill, the Captain was ready to explode. When the Sergeant finally arrived back at the mill the Captain told him to rig the kegs to explode when the troops were about ten minutes away. The explosion was fairly impressive but the damage was not all that bad and could have been repaired in normal times. The wheel, grinding stones, and all the gears were twisted and broken. Brick was scattered everywhere. The first floor of stone was still in place.

The mill site is private property today and few folks know the location. When I visit the site I can still see the wanton destruction that was perpetrated by the U.S. Army. The loss of that mill brought on near starvation for the civilians in that area. It was a war crime pure and simple.

The Coleman family suffered the loss of their fortune during the war. There were no funds left to rebuild the mill. The family also lost a son named Aylett Coleman whose body lies in the Coleman graveyard at Wintergreen. Two other sons Walker and Steve made it all the way through the war and was at the Surrender in Appomattox. The Coleman Family also lost all their labor causing Wintergreen to cease as a plantation.

That old mill site is important to me because there used to be an old Colored Mammy named Aunt Mildred who lived there in a log cabin. I can remember going there with my mother to see Aunt Mildred. While they talked I would play with the bricks laying all around her yard and she would give me a coffee with a lot of milk and she would always say "Don't go near the creek".

GRIST MILLS ON SPRUCE CREEK

THE SECOND

After the loss of the brick mill, the folks in the South Rockfish Valley were devastated. Ground corn was not only human food but it was used to feed livestock. It was almost as important as salt. The people needed a mill but none could afford to build one. They had just come through war and there was little money for anything.

In the year 1870, there was a great storm that stuck in Virginia that some would say was worse than the storm named Camille in 1969. Due to the lack of information in 1870, no one really know the whole story of the devastation visited on Virginia. A great many lives and property were lost during that storm.

After that storm, two men named Slaughter and Fitzpatrick arrived at Wintergreen. They had heard that there was property for sale. Some of the property they bought was the site of the old brick mill and the property where 151, Glen Thorne Lane, and Spruce Creek Lane meet.

One of the things they wanted to do first was to construct a grist mill as they realized how badly it was needed. After all the storm damage they decided that the old brick mill site was too much in the path of storms. As the war was over they weren't worried about the Yankee army anymore but the weather had to be taken into consideration.

They decided that the best place to build the new mill was at the corner of what is now Glen Thorne Lane and Rt 151. You have to remember that this was in the 1870s and the lay of the land has changed a lot.

Slaughter and Fitzpatrick had decided that they did not want to invest a lot of money in this mill. The mill house was to be built of wood frame and the wheel was to be wood, They knew the gears would last longer made of metal. These parts were contracted out and construction began.

Folks were wondering how they would get water to the mill. Slaughter and Fitzpatrick had this all figured out. They simply extended the raceway from the old brick mill. Of course, they had to dig another holding pond but those boys were engineers and they got a raceway to the new mill by digging a raceway into the side of a hill.

Even though the mill no longer exists the raceway and waterworks are still there. It was an amazing feat and I visit it often to be reminded of what those old boys could do with strings and sticks for survey gear. The raceway still exists today and could be used with very little work.

This mill operated until around 1954 and had a few different owners. There was Tom Truslow, Bob Hughes, Alec Hughes (My Grandfather), and Grover Harris.

Grover Harris and his wife Katherine ran the General Store along with the mill. The store is the same building that houses the Nature Museum today. Katherine ran the store and was also the Post Mistress. As a small child, I can remember walking down to the Post Office to pick up our mail and on my way, I would stop and talk to my Uncle Moses (Bunk) and Aunt Lottie. They love to tell scary stories to little children. Uncle Bunk would tell me about Katherine being a witch and that she could turn me into a tadpole. Lottie would talk about the Old Ragman who lived between their house and the store. I was a nervous wreck when I got back home and my father would tell me not to pay any attention to Bunk and Lottie cause they were lunatics and should be in the mental hospital but just in case he told me to be careful walking down that road cause Uncle Bunk and Lottie could be right.

Grover Harris and his four brothers were all drunks. His four brothers were all unmarried and lived in the Wintergreen house. Grover and his wife Katherine lived above the store. She ran the store and Post Office. He operated the mill. and drank all the time. A grist mill can be a dangerous place even for the careful and sober person. Grover found that out the hard way.

The mill had an overshot wheel which meant water to make it turn poured out of a water box built on top of the wheel frame. During the fall of the year when leaves fell, the water box would fill up with dead leaves and someone had to climb up on a ladder and clean the leaves out. It was a job that normally a sober person would undertake. Grover, in his infinite wisdom, decided to do it himself while in his normal drunken state and save some money. He climbed up on the water box, lost his balance, and fell in head-first onto the turning wheel.

Grover made Katherine a widow that day. I think she was relieved as she had spent many a long year with the drunken Grover. Katherine kept the store and Post Office running but the mill never ground another pound of corn.

The mill sat abandoned until Peter Agelasto bought the property and donated the wheel and gears to the Wintergreen resort where it was on display until recently the resort changed its motif and brought the wheel and gears back down to Wintergreen where we hope someday to put it on display.

MEDICAL CARE AT WINTERGREEN IN THE 1890s

This story was written by my Uncle Emmett
Rittenhouse. He and my father Tucker Hughes were about
the same age and their stories of life at Wintergreen
matched very closely. It is a sad story that will make you
glad you live in a whole different world. This story takes
place just over a hundred years ago. We have come a long
way. The first part deals with justice. The story is how
Uncle Emmett told it.

Where the road crossed the river going to Adial was a
dangerous ford when the water was up. The ford was
named Nellysford because before the war a girl named
Nelly was thrown from her horse there and drowned.

On the ridge above were the Post Office and a store
where Mr. Warrick had been murdered during the war by
Jesse Lowe. Jesse Lowe called him out one night after
closing time on the pretense of buying something. Jesse
Lowe knocked Mr. Warrick in the head with a plow point.
Jesse was caught a few days later and he confessed to
committing the crime. Jesse was immediately hung from
the limb of a large oak tree in the store yard without the
benefit of a judge or jury. This was Wintergreen Justice at
its best.

Nellysford was very treacherous. I have seen Papa cross
it when the water was so high that it would almost run over
the horses' back. He would throw up his legs on the horse's
neck to keep from getting his boots wet and then the water
would lap up against the saddle. A strong horse could ford
it all right but if he was lazy and gave way to the current it
would wash him away downstream. Papa knew how to ford
it by starting in the ford several yards above the road on the
other side so that if the horse was washed down a little that
he would strike the road on the other side. One day papa

was riding a horse named Old Rock. Old Rock was a lazy old horse and he gave way to the water current and he passed the landing place. Old Rock and Papa were washed downstream for a quarter mile before he could find a place to climb out of the river. I don't know how papa ever escaped being drowned for he took a lot of chances for a man with only one leg.

Opposite the store was a small brick house that was built by old Doctor Coleman for his office and he used it for many years. When he died and the estate was divided up it was bought by a young Doctor named Doctor Fitzpatrick who used it for his office. He never married but had an old white woman named Mrs. Goolsby keep house for him. He lived as he pleased.

Dr. Fitzpatrick had two old hounds that followed him everywhere he went and slept on the bed with him at night. He thought a great deal of these dogs and no matter what they did he did not want you to do anything to them or complain about them. He came to our house once and they were with him. Miss Susan, the old lady that kept house for us knew how bad they were and she kept all the doors shut to keep them out. In an unguarded moment, she left the dining room door open and one of them sneaked in. When Miss Susan came back he leaped across the table and swiped a pound of butter and never touched the table. He kept on running and when he came to the front door and found that closed he jumped through the side window and took out all the glass and sash.

Dr. Fitzpatrick was very picturesque on horseback. He rode a rawboned old plow horse that looked just like the one that Don Quixote rode. He wore a long frock coat that split in the middle and one tail was on each side of the saddle. He wore stovepipe boots in summer and winter. He would rid along with one of his pants legs all the way down and the other hung up on his boot, the two old hounds following along on each side of his horse.

Dr. Fitzpatrick chewed tobacco all the time and his long white whiskers were stained by tobacco juice. The juice ran out of both corners of his mouth and down on his beard staining it amber. He also liked to suck raw eggs and the yellow would run down and mix with the tobacco juice. This was not really out of the ordinary as most men chewed tobacco. It was a habit that you still see at times.

Dr. Fitzpatrick was more interested in hunting and fishing than in medicine. He rode through the wood and up and down the river all of the time. He never carried a doctor's bag. He did carry a few pills in his vest pocket and when he pulled a pill out o his pocket it was just as apt to be a grubworm as a pill.

I was over at Gannaway's once and I had a very large boil over my eye. It had been there some time and was very painful and I could not see out of that eye for more than two weeks. Mrs. Gannaway told me to get Doctor Fitzpatrick to lance it for me. The Doctor was out on the store porch and I asked him if he could fix the boil. He reached down in his pocket and drew out an old rusty knife and sharpened it on the bottom of his boot. He took hold of the back of my head and sliced the boil open and about a half cup of yellow liquid poured out. He didn't have any disinfectant so he poured some of Gannaway's brandy on the boil and it healed up with no problem. He told me that when I got some money I could buy him a drink to replace what he had poured on the boil.

Doctor Fitzpatrick spent a lot of time hanging around Gannaway's stills at Wintergreen because they had plenty of apple brandy. A lot of folks would trade brandy for medical advice or first aid treatment on the spot after a fight. Gannaway contended that he could hold a pint of brandy in front of Doctor Fitzpatrick and lead him to hell.

I remember one time the Doctor came riding by our house. he had a dead wild cat tied to his saddle and wanted me to go coon hunting with him. Papa said it would be all right so I saddled a horse and we rode up on the mountain and got off the horses and had a seat on the ground. The Doctor had an old coon hound named Rowdy. Old Rowdy wandered off into the woods like he was looking for a coon trail. Old Rowdy started off like he was seriously searching for a coon trail. After about an hour of sitting in the leaves talking, not hearing Old Rowdy bark, we figured he must have treed a coon down in a hollow and we couldn't hear him bark. As we didn't have any idea where to look for Old Rowdy we decided to go home and get up early to begin the search for Old Rowdy and his treed coon. We only walked a few yards and there was Old Rowdy curled up in a pile of leaves. Old Rowdy got up and followed us home. He had no intention of chasing after a coon all night.

I don't suppose that Doctor Fitzpatrick had read a medical book for forty years when I knew him but he was so sympathetic, kind, good, and liked to talk to people. He was a good listener and would give free medical advice. Everybody liked him. He hardly ever got paid in cash money but took his pay in a piece of meat, a bushel of corn, or a load of hay for his horse Old Bonney. Most of the people didn't pay him anything. He had no idea how much anybody owed him because he didn't keep any books. He would make house calls whenever or whoever asked rich or poor, high or low, white or black and never ask about pay. He just took whatever they gave him.

I remember that he had been attending an old one-legged Confederate and his family for a long time. The old man had gotten hold of a little money when he sold his tobacco crop and went to pay the Doctor. He handed two five-dollar bills to Doctor Fitzpatrick and the Doctor handed him one five-dollar bill back and spoke. "Zack, I wouldn't keep these five dollars but I am just bound to have a little money to buy Old Bonney some corn and hay".

My father sent for Doctor Fitzpatrick when my stepmother was close to having her baby. He was getting old then and did not know anything about delivering babies. but my father wanted him there because he had been the family Doctor for many years and the. Doctor Fitzpatrick called in Doctor Garth who was as old as him and had been out of practice for years. When Doctor Garth arrived, he opened his medical bag to get his bottle of brandy and I saw his medical instruments. They were so rusty I couldn't tell what they were. They couldn't have been used or cleaned for years. They were not fit for any use.

It was the last days of January that my stepmother was taken sick and she died on the 7th day of February. Those two old Doctors just sat there in the parlor by the fireplace and let her die as they did not know what to do. I am not trying to say anything against them, I am just trying to describe how crude and ignorant people were in that day. The Doctors were used to having a midwife take care of births. They usually just showed up and waited until it was over.

They stayed on for a few days until the midwife told them that my stepmother was at death's door. The two old Doctors said they did not like to watch people die and they had finished off all the brandy. The patient was dying, the brandy was all gone and they did not see any use in staying any longer.

DOCTOR JOHN COLEMAN EVERETTE of "UPLAND"

Credit for this story goes to my Aunt Daisy's husband, Uncle Emmett Rittenhouse. Uncle Emmett did not use paragraphs and neither will I in this story. It was told as if he was talking to his friends sitting on an old oak stump.

Dr. Everette was kin to the Coleman family of Wintergreen and when he finished Medical School at the University of Virginia, they asked him to come to the Rockfish Valley to help Dr. Fitch with the Diphtheria Epidemic that was raging among the children. Dr. Fitch was getting old and he asked Dr. Everette to stay on and replace him as the Doctor for the Rockfish Valley. Dr. Everette was a very wild and dashing young man. Where there was a party or dance you would find Dr. Everette having a great time and also partaking in a drink or two. As fate would have it he soon met and fell in love with a very beautiful young girl named Nellie Martin whose father owned a large Estate down by LODEBAR. They lived in a log cabin at Lodebar that Dr. Everette also used as an office. Most of Dr. Everette's practice was done on horseback making house calls. In those days a doctor wasn't called for until the patient was bedridden. After the Epidemic was over and he got settled in Dr. Fitch was still practicing and they were soon in competition and they soon became political and personal enemies. Dr. Fitch was the Delegate to the state Legislature and Dr. Everette ran against him several times and finally beat him. I remember one election that I thought was pathetic, both of them at the Slaughter (Wintergreen) precinct electioneering. Dr. Everette is young, haughty, and proud, and poor Dr. Fitch is old, gray, goodhearted, and kind. While Dr. Everette, when making house calls always wanted to know who would pay, and Dr, Fitch would make house calls without thinking of pay. He would take a basket of turnips if the family had no money. Everybody at Slaughter's seemed to be for Dr. Everette and he walked around waving a handful of greenbacks and wanted to bet anybody that he would beat old Dr, Fitch. Everything seemed to be going Dr. Everette's way. Old Dr. Fitch was walking around looking very sad and hurt to think that the people he had Doctored for years receiving no better pay than a bushel of corn or a side of meat should turn against him. Old man, Zack Phillips couldn't stand it any longer so he borrowed $50.00 from one of his boys and bet Dr. Everette that old Dr. Fitch would beat him. Old Man Zack Phillips was a one-legged Civil War Veteran and they use to call him "Turk the 49" because he belonged to the 49th Virginia Regiment during the war and it was said he fought like a Turk. It was several days before the vote was counted and the first news was that Dr. Everette had won. The old Turk was really sad because he didn't know where he would get the money to pay his boy back. He told his boy that he should have known that old Dr. Fitch was played out and that he ought to have had more sense than to have bet on him. A few days later we got word that Dr. Fitch had beaten Dr. Everette more than two to one. The precinct at Slaughter was the only one that Dr. Everette carried. Dr. Everette ran against Dr. Fitch a few more times until he finally beat him. Hub Martin had held the stakes and when the Old Turk went to collect his money, he was one of the happiest men we ever saw. After a few weeks, The Old Turk (Zack Phillips) and Dr. Everette met at the Slaughter Post Office and they got to quarreling. Dr. Everette abused The Old Turk and cussed him several times. The Old Turk had but one good leg and walked on crutches but he was a powerful man physically. The Old Turk threw the crutches away and grabbed Dr. Everette around the neck with his arms and they fell backward to the ground and he held a vice-like grip on Dr. Everette's neck with his left arm and beat him in the face with his right hand and as Dr. Everette could not extricate himself from this death-like grip he had to call for help to get away from the Old Turk. They say he had the most powerful grip in his hands and arms of any man around Slaughter. It was as if nature gave him this gift to compensate for the loss of his leg. Dr. Everette never crossed the Old Turk again but developed a great respect for the Old Turk.

D. Everette was a very strange man. Before he got married, he was a wild and wicked man but after he got married he settled down considerably. He fathered five children, four boys, and one girl that he thought a lot of. A preacher named Mr. Howard held a week-long meeting at the Rockfish Presbyterian Church and Dr. Everette joined the church and seemed to be a completely changed man. He attended church for a while and seemed to take some interest in it. Mr. Howard ended up preaching every day for several weeks and he stirred up the people very much. Mr. Howard was very bitter against the use of tobacco, whiskey, coffee, and tea. He maintained that was what was the matter with women they were drunk on coffee and tea so a lot of folks gave up these things and joined the church. Dr. Everette oldest boy that he thought so much of and intended to send him to college to become a doctor died suddenly. The grief over the death of this boy upset the Doctors mind and he quit going to church and railed against God. He lost interest in his other children. They attended the local school but none went on to college. After this, the only time he was known to give credit to God for anything was when John Ryland Coleman shot him. Dr. Everette and John Ryland had married sisters. John Ryland Coleman was known to have a hot temper and he had heard that Dr. Everette had made some ungentlemanly remarks about his wife. One cold wet day late in November John Ryland Coleman came riding up to Lodebar where Woods Witt kept a store and Post Office. He got off his horse and left him standing with the bridle reins thrown over the pommel of the saddle and came into the store. He saw Dr. Everette sitting on a nail keg. Dr. Everette made some unkind remarks to John Ryland. John Ryland always carried two forty-four pistols in his hip pockets. He pulled one out and started shooting at Dr. Everette as he ran into a back store room trying to escape but fell over a wooden box. John Ryland shot all six bullets but Dr. Everette showed no signs of being hit. He was wrestling Dr. Everette and was unable to get an aimed shot off. John Ryland jumped up off of Dr. Everette and thinking he had wounded Dr. Everette and took off. He made his escape and jumped on his horse and left the scene of the crime in a sweeping gallop. John rode straight to the Court House to consult with his lawyer and cousin Tinsley Coleman. Tinsley advised him to leave the county for a while until things settled down. John Ryland made his way to relatives in Kentucky after a few years before returning home. John Rylan didn't realize it but Dr. Everette was not seriously hurt. He was wearing a heavy overcoat and John Rylan was pressing the pistol so hard against the ribs that the pistol turned sideways and the bullets hit the ribs and did not penetrate the body. After staying away for a few years the old wounds and hatred healed up and on account of the kinship of the families, Dr. Everette agreed that John Ryland could come back and he would not prosecute him. They were first cousins and had married sisters. John Ryland came back but never did have much to do with each other. Dr. Everette was always afraid of John Rylan, although he himself was a tough, bold man John Rylan was just a little too tough for him.

Doctor Everette Stories

Dr. Everette used to tell a tale about an old Confederate Veteran that came to his office to ask him to fill out his papers so he could draw his pension. His name was John Coffey and he lived up on the Blue Ridge Mountain about fifteen miles from Dr. Everette's Office. The Doctor said the old man came walking in one morning before breakfast. The Doctor examined him after breakfast and found out that the old man had everything medically a man could have and live. Dr. Everette thought that if he had seen the old man at home in his own bed, he would have sworn that the old man would not live through the day. After the examination, Dr. Everette became curious to know more about him. He knew the old man had walked fifteen miles to his office so he asked him what he was going to do now. Old man Coffey told the Doctor that he had a daughter living over on Taylor's Creek and would stop there for dinner (lunch) and then head back home. Dr. Everette knew that Taylor's Creek was five miles in the opposite direction. The Doctor then asked Old Man Coffey what he was going to do after visiting his daughter. Old Man Coffey spit out a long stream of tobacco juice that curved around the stovepipe and landed in the sandbox under the stove. "Well," Old Man Coffey said, "I reckon I'll get on back home then". So that would be forty miles of walking that day for a man Dr. Everette thought could not live an hour longer. Old man Coffee got his pension and lived quite a few years longer.

Doctor Everette's Breakfast

One morning an old farmer from up on the mountain, before the sun was up stopped by the doctor's office and wanted the Doctor to give him some medicine that would help his appetite. The Doctor invited the old man to eat breakfast with him and the old man ate a very hearty breakfast. After eating they went back to the office. The Doctor asked the old man about the mountain people and how they were getting along. They talked for a long time about various things but neither one of them said anything about the medicine that he came for. When the old man got up and started to leave, he turned back and said "Can you give me some pills for my appetite?" The doctor said, " I noticed you eating at breakfast and didn't notice anything wrong with your appetite as you ate a large hearty breakfast. I don't think you need any pills for your appetite." The old man replied, "Oh yes Doctor I can eat what you had for breakfast, hot biscuits fried ham and eggs, jelly and coffee, but I want the pills to make me eat what I have at home".

Doctor Parson

The closest dentist to Wintergreen was Dr. Parsons who owned Pharsalia Plantation over at Massie's Mill. Dr. Parsons was from West Virginia. When he finished school, he set up a practice in Lynchburg and worked there for about 20 years building up a good practice and saving his money.

Pharsalia was a large plantation in Massie's Mill. It had been owned by William Massie. At about this time, the Plantation was changing over from tobacco to apple orchards. When Dr. parsons heard it was up for sale he bought it and moved from Lynchburg and began farming. He kept up his dentistry practice with an office at Pharsalia and patients from Amherst County to the Rockfish Valley came to him. The only reason he kept the dentistry office was that he liked it and he liked having company.

When people had to travel a long distance to see a dentist in those days they usually had put it off so long that they had a lot of work. It would sometimes take a week or two to have all the work done. Dr. Parsons only took one patient at a time. He would work on that patient for an hour or so in the morning after breakfast and another hour or so after lunch. The patient could spend his time reading in the library or walking about the place. One old man said he spent two weeks there and when Doctor Parson finished the bill came to $32.00, but Doctor Parsons knew he was a poor man and only charged him $20.00. Another old man went to Doctor Parsons and got a lot of fillings. Forty years later he still had them.

Old Man Gannaway

Old Man Gannaway lived down at Old Wintergreen back in the early 1900s. I don't remember anybody referring to him as anything other than Old Man Gannaway. He had the piece of land between the grist mill and Spruce Creek and lived in what was known as the Brady house in the back right beside Spruce Creek. The house burned down back in the '60s but the field rock chimney still stands.

Old Man Gannaway was quite the entrepreneur. He built a store that burned down, then he tried a sawmill. He finally hit the jackpot by building a still which was legal back then. Apples were becoming a big money crop and to Od Man Gannaway's mind, the only logical thing to do with apples was to make brandy. Apples didn't store very well if you didn't have cold storage and apples in those days were usually all scabby and wormy. The easiest thing was to make brandy. It wasn't long before Old Man Gannaway had four distilleries going.

Old man Gannaway's permit allowed him to sell his brandy by the barrel or gallon. He was not allowed to sell it by the drink. Of course, most folks up there could only afford it by the drink. Old Man Gannaway came up with the perfect solution. He would sell you a gallon but he would hold the gallon and you paid him the cost of a drink every time you took one. Most of the men up there had a gallon going all the time. Mind you, this was not legal.

At about this time, bare-knuckle fighting got popular. John L. Sullivan was the hero of all the young men white and black. When the mail was delivered there at Wintergreen on Saturday there would be a great crowd hanging around waiting for the newspaper to find out what

John L. Sullivan was doing. This was good for Old Man Gannaway's business.

Bare-Knuckle Boxing was popular among the young black men of the community and there would be a lot of matches fought and a great deal of betting. Now, when the black men fought and one got knocked down the other would stand back and let him up. If he made the count the fight would resume.

This was not so with the white men. There was a bad man there named Tom Truslow. When a man fought Tom and went down Tom was on top of him. He was fighting Walter Quick and Walter faltered a bit. This was what Tom was waiting for. Tom reared back and with a mighty left, he knocked Walter down. Walter was game and tried to get up but Tom was on him. Tom was able to get close enough to bite Walker in the lower lip. He tore Walter's lip about half off. That ended the fight.

Dr. Everette happened to be in the crowd. He poured some brandy on Walter's lip and sewed it back on, but it didn't take and got infected so Dr. Everette cut it off and poor Walter was one fearsome-looking soul the rest of his life.

Old Dow Thompson was another fierce fighter around Old Wintergreen. He was meaner than Tom Truslow it was said. When Dow heard, what Tom had done to Walter Quick he went looking for Tom. They locked horns there in front of the grist mill. They hit and wrestled each other till finally, Dow got Tom down. When the dust cleared a little Tom was on top. This is where Dow made a fatal mistake, he stuck his thumb in Tom's mouth. Tom bit down and you hear the bone cracked and gristle being stretched. When Dow finally got his hand back he was missing a thumb and Tom was sitting there chewing on it. They say that when he got it chewed down to a wad he swallowed it. Dr. Everette was there and he borrowed some Brandy from Old Man Gannaway and soaked Dow's Hand in it and wrapped it in a clean rag. A few days later when the hand didn't get infected Old Man Gannaway charged him for the brandy.

Nobody ever knew who reported him but it was the general opinion that it had to be somebody's wife or some do-gooder that attended the old clapboard church over in John Harris's field. They knew it wasn't a Harris cause they all had a gallon going over at the still. With the brandy by the drink and all the fighting, the Sheriff from Lovingston had to come over and look into the situation.

You have to remember that in those days there was a lot of commotion about alcohol. It was called the Temperance Movement There were a lot of church ladies and crooked politicians (as if there were any other kinds) involved so they were pushing the Sheriff. The sheriff and his people searched every inch of Old Man Gannaway's property and found over a hundred barrels buried, in barns, and other outbuildings.

The Sheriff had to bring 20 horse-drawn wagons to haul the brandy barrels over to Rockfish Depot where it was loaded on a train and sent to Richmond.

The thing I find strange or not was the fact that Old Man Gannaway was not arrested nor were his stills destroyed. When the next crop of apples came in he was back in business with two more to distill corn. No doubt Old Man Gannaway was a successful businessman.

Old Winter Green Stories

The Property Line

Alec Hughes and Sally Napier were married in the early 1880s on Spruce Creek. For the first couple of years, they lived on the Pharsalia Plantation at Massies Mill where Alec served as Overseer.

With the help of his father John J. Hughes, Alec was finally able to buy some land on Spruce Creek where he built a house beside a nice spring whose run-off creek served as the property line between Alec and the Coleman Family.

Apples were the big crop at this time. Tobacco had fallen out of favor due to its tendency to drain the flatlands of its ability to grow money crops. Apples became the new money crop because apples grew best on hillsides and Old Winter Green had an abundance of hillsides.

Alec planted apple orchards on his property and did very well. His crops went into the making of apple brandy in the four distilleries run by a Mr. Gannaway at Wintergreen whom everyone called Old Man Gannaway. Alec got appointed Magistrate and postmaster. He also owned a store and a grist mill at Old Winter Green.

The Colemans sold their land to the Harris family in 1900. This transaction took a few months to complete. The creek that divided Alec and the Coleman land took a curve over into Alec's land. He was looking at it one day and it occurred to him that if he dug a canal for the creek along the side of Coleman's mountain and changed the path of the creek he would gain around three acres of flat bottom land. He figured nobody would even notice before the deal was done between the Colemans and Harris.

It took about a year for Coleman and Harris to complete the sale and there was no survey because neither side wanted to pay a surveyor. Alec noticed all the confusion going on between the Coleman family and John Harris. He took his time and dug his canal changing the property line.

When John Harris finally noticed that the creek had been re-routed, he made a complaint to the Court at Lovingston. Over the years the Court at Lovingston had been involved in many problems and complaints about the Harris family. They were in court frequently about property arguments, fist fighting, shootings, public drunkenness, and otherwise a very disagreeable crowd. The court was tired of dealing with local problems at Winter Green. The Court decided that this case should be handled at the Magistrates Hearing at Wintergreen.

This showed how devious Alec could be and how wise he was to have friends in the Lovingston Court. Alec happened to be the Magistrate at Winter Green. When the case came up it was held on the porch of Alec's grist mill at Winter Green. This was a big event at Winter Green and drew a great crowd. It wasn't often that arguments between the Harris, Colemans, and Hughes were settled in this type of public way. Personal problems were usually settled privately with a fistfight in the woods or a shot from a distance landing within inches of the opposite family member's head. This time Alec decided to settle the problem legally.

On the date that Alec had chosen, the crowd was gathered in front of the Grist Mill. All morning Old Man Gannaway had one of his distilleries distributing Apple Brandy to the crowd paid for by Alec. Most of the folks didn't like the Colemans or the Harris families so they were on Alec's side. Alec would have made a great politician. He gave credit at his store and would make sure every customer at his mill received extra corn meal because he knew most had little else to eat. Alec made sure nobody went hungry if he could help. It was understood by all that his wife Sally was behind his generosity.

Alec came out on the mill porch all dressed up in his black suit, wearing his stovepipe boots and an old pistol in his belt. He called the Magistrate's Hearing to order and explained the main points of the case. John Harris stated his case by accusing Alec of stealing his land by re-routing the creek that was the property line and he objected to Alec being the Magistrate to hear the case as he was also the defendant.

Alec told John Harris that as the duly appointed Magistrate, he would be hearing the case and that there was no legal reason that a Magistrate could not hold a hearing against himself. Alec also explained to John Harris that he could withdraw his complaint and they could settle this like gentlemen. John Harris was a poor shot and a coward who declined the invitation and agreed to accept the Magistrate Hearing's decision.

Alec finally got the crowd settled down and delivered his decision. He said the creek in its old bed was constantly overflowing its banks and flooding the three acres turning it into a swamp. Alec had recently built his new home on a hill above the creek and in the summer the swamp mosquitos were making it almost impossible to live there. He had the new waterway dug deeper and in a straight line giving that swampy land better drainage and doing away with the mosquito hatchery. Alec also noted that the creek was still the property line no matter where it flowed. He had not changed the survey that had stood for a hundred years originally surveyed by Hawes Coleman just after the first war with England. The Magistrate's decision, in this case, went for Alec Hughes.

All the Hughes family that have lived there agree that those three acres made one of the finest vegetable gardens in the area and I agree as I ate from that garden for the first eighteen years of my life. Grand Father Alec was brilliant.

As time went on the Harris family refused to let the property line disagreement rest. Whenever Hughes and Harris met there would be harsh words and usually, a gun or knife was involved. No one was killed but there were lots of injuries on both sides. Neither side would travel alone at night for years and even today, while most have forgotten, there are a couple who remember the stories.

The Murder Trial at WINTERGREEN

When Alec Hughes was Magistrate at Wintergreen the Magisterial District covered from Brents Mountain to Nellysford. Alec held Magistrate Hearings on the porch of his grist mill at Wintergreen. If the hearing was for a minor offense Alec handled it at Magistrate's Hearing but more serious cases were taken to the higher court at Lovingston.

There had been hard feelings about Lovingston that went back to the early 1800's when Nelson County was created by being broken off from Amherst County thereby moving the Court from Amherst to the new county seat at Lovingston bringing the law closer to the Rockfish Valley, and Wintergreen. The folks in the Rockfish Valley liked to keep the law at a distance. Alec liked to poke the Court at Lovingston in the eye every chance he got.

It was in the early summer when Alec was at his Grist Mill grinding corn into meal. Two men walked into the mill and asked if they could speak to Alec outside where it was quiet. When Alec walked out on the porch, there was a wagon at the hitching post with a woman and four kids sitting back in the load box. The woman had her hands tied behind her.

One of the men told Alec that they lived up on the mountain above Cub Creek. The men explained to Alec that the woman's husband had come home drunk the night before. He had beaten the woman and children. Then went to bed and passed out. The woman then got a butcher knife from the kitchen and cut her husband's throat while he lay drunk in bed covered in blood from the beating, he had given his wife. She then got her children together and went to the neighbor's home and told him what she had done.

The two men told Alec that they knew this was going on

for a long time but were afraid of the husband and had not reported it. The man was big and mean. Nobody wanted to cross him. He had been creating havoc up in the Beech Grove neighborhood for years. It took his poor wife to do what needed to be done. She was afraid for herself and her kids.

Alec didn't know what to do at first. He had never had anything like this come before him. While thinking about what to do he told the two men to take the woman and her kids to his wife Sally up on Spruce Creek while he decided what to do. Alec knew that this was a capital case that should go before the Judge at Lovingston but Alec would rather do the right thing rather than send it to Lovingston where who knows which way it would go with a Jury trial. The husband was from a large family that had kinfolk all over the county and Alec didn't want to take the chance that some of his kin might get on the Jury.

The next day Alec took some of his sons and they rode horseback up to the cabin above Cub Creek in Beech Grove. As they rode up to the cabin there were buzzards perched on the roof and they could hear dogs inside. The horses were very nervous and hard to handle. Once they tied off the horses they went into the cabin. There was a bed in the corner and four or five dogs were fighting over what was on the bed.

Alec's son Tucker got a big chunk of wood and beat the dogs off. They had been eating the husband's remains. Alec had his sons wrapped the remains in some rags and took them out in the woods where they dug a grave and buried him. The Hughes boys had no kind words or request for forgiveness for what they considered no more than trash stuffed into a hole in the ground.

Alec told his sons to clean up the cabin and it was the

spring of the year he had them bring a plow up to the cabin and plow a garden. He also told them to plant a garden for the widow and her kids.

The next day was Saturday when most folks around Wintergreen came to get corn meal and other store-bought goods. Alec decided to hold the widow's trial. He had thought long and hard about this. He wanted a big crowd to make sure all the citizens knew the facts. He had already decided that this was Wintergreen's business, not Lovingston's or Richmond's.

At noon the crowd gathered and Alec stepped out on the mill porch. He was wearing his black stovepipe boots and a black suit with his old pistol holstered on his right side. Alec explained to the crowd what had happened and he brought the widow up on the porch and had her tell her side of it. It didn't take long because everyone already knew the story. The neighbors were all there with their heads hanging down in shame because they all knew the kind of treatment the widow had endured and had done nothing about it. Alec talked about the responsibility a neighbor had for his neighbor. He spoke about the inhumanity that would cause a neighbor to ignore a neighbor in trouble.

After Alec finished his speechifying, he told the crowd that the next person he heard of treating his family in an inhumane manner would answer for it with a visit from the Magistrates posse, whose members were Alec's sons and nephews.

Alec told the widow that she was to return home and raise her children without any feelings of guilt. If she was to have any problems, especially with her husband's family she was to send a message by one of her children to Alec.

I didn't name the family because I am sure they would

be embarrassed by the story. My Grandfather Alec Hughes was one of the most honest, upright citizens that the Rockfish valley has ever produced. With no training in the law, he was able to apply the law at Wintergreen for many years and I have heard not one real complaint about his decisions.

It was part of Alex's job as magistrate to record births and deaths. There was one lady that I knew whose birth date was recorded wrong and she complained to every Hughes she met. That was the only complaint I have heard and that was administrative.

Turk The Forty-Nine

This story was told by Uncle Emmett Rittenhouse. Turk the Forty-Nine was Zachariah Phillips. Others from Wintergreen who served Virginia during the War of Northern Aggression include Walker Coleman, Steve Coleman, John Jacob Meeks (Who carried Henry Rittenhouse off the field of Battle at Fishers' Hill), Henry Rittenhouse, John Hughes, John Wills Harris. Sam Coleman, Ayellette Coleman (Killed at Fisher's Hill)

There once lived in the neighborhood of Wintergreen a worthy gentleman who was called either "Old Turk" or "Turk the Forty Nine" as he had fought in the War under Stonewall Jackson in the Forty-Ninth Virginia Regiment. It was said they called him the "old Turk" because he fought like a Turk against the Yankees.

The Old Turk lost his leg at Gettysburg. He walked with the aid of homemade crutches for the rest of his life. The Surgeons had cut his leg off close up to the hip making it too difficult to walk with a wooden leg hence, crutches were his only options. He used to ride an old skinny nag with his crutches laid across his lap over the saddle and with his leg cut off so high up, it made him look like he was riding sidesaddle like a woman. Even with his handicap, he was a good-natured, jolly old fellow full of life and enthusiasm.

When the Old Turk returned from the war, he married a girl that had promised him marriage before the war and she would not go back on her word. They lived in another part of the county until his wife's parents died. She inherited a small place near Wintergreen and came there to live.

Although the Old Turk was unable to do much farm work he was able to work and supervise his sons in the growing of tobacco and corn. They were hard-working boys and they loved their father and followed everything he said. When they moved to Wintergreen the word spread pretty quickly that even though being poor white folks they would succeed through hard work and perseverance.

In the late 1890's Glenthorne was owned by a man named Alfred Harris who also owned Glen Mary. Mr. Harris lived at Glen Mary and hired Henry Rittenhouse to manage Glenthorne. Mr. Harris gave Henry Rittenhouse full authority to hire hands and to rent cropland to tenants as he chose. Mr. Harris had full faith in Henry Rittenhouse as a farm manager. He never changed any things that Henry did.

Henry had made a habit to rent land to colored folks only because they tended to accept his decisions more readily than white renters, but when The Old Turk approached Henry to rent land he did not hesitate. Both Henry and The Old Turk had been in the war and both had lost a leg. There is and always will be a feeling of brotherhood between soldiers and they tend to help each other when needed. The Old Turk also had three of the hardest working boys that ever were up in that part of the country and Henry wanted to help them to make a start in life as they were so ambitious to get on in the world. (I would state here that as a small child, I knew one of those boys when he was old man. It was John Phillips and he was bedridden at the time. My mother had been a nurse and she would visit to give him his shots. I used to sit in his room and talk to him as a small child. It has been a fond memory.)

The Old Turk's status at Glenthorne was not an enviable one. There were more than a hundred colored people working there. Some were hired fieldhands and some sharecropped or rented land. The colored people didn't think much of The Old Turk as they saw him and his boys as competition. They looked down on him and viewed him and his boys as poor white trash.

The sons of The Old Turk were hard workers and they made good crops on the rented land at Glenthorne but with all the competition there was very little profit. To help out The Old Turk taught the small colored school. The school lasted only a few months of the year during the winter when it was too cold to work the fields. The school only paid about ten dollars a month. His wife took in sewing and gave The Old Turk everything she made.

The Old Turk was a great drunkard and most of their money went into John Gannaway's pocket for apple brandy over at the Wintergreen still. His wife soon found out that she had made a great mistake by marrying him but by then it was much too late. She was a good woman and stayed with him.

The Old Turk was a rough, aggressive, profane man, although a good man in his own way. He never went to church or made any profession of religion. His wife was a meek mild woman that never crossed him in any way and she thought that everything he did was right. He was a great character; he would wake up in the morning at about four o'clock and crow like a rooster to wake the boys up so they could get to work. He was hard on them and worked them hard in the fields even though they were small boys. His children all loved him though, and thought there was nobody like their Pappy.

If The Old Turk didn't come home at night, they would go out in search of him. They would usually find him lying beside the road drunk. They would push and shove him up in the saddle and one would lead the horse and one would get on each side of the horse to hold him in the saddle and in this way they would get him home. Even with all his faults, those boys thought their old Pappy was the greatest man in the world.

The three boys that he brought to Glenthorn to make a crop with were young, one was ten years, one was thirteen years old and the other was fifteen, but they were already hard workers. Where others boys of that age thought about play, these boys thought about work.

The Old Turk couldn't work in the fields but he could ride horseback and drive a wagon. He obtained the contract on carrying mail from Slaughter's (Wintergreen) to the Afton train depot six days a week for one hundred and fifty dollars a year. He worked this route for about years. while his boys worked the fields.

The Old Turk decided that he wanted to attend the commencement exercises at the University of Virginia in 1895. He picked up Emmett Rittenhouse who was just a boy to ride with him to Afton on the mail run and then took the train to Charlottesville. Where they heard William Jennings Bryan give a lecture at the commencement address entitled "Jefferson Still Lives". It was the greatest day of Emmett's life as he had never been away from Glenthorn before.

The day was hot and the Old Turk filled up every pocket with pints of whiskey and would stop and lean against every lamppost he saw to take a drink. He never got totally drunk, just enough to make him talk and be funny, and to tell everyone that he was Turk the Forty Nine.

There were a lot of old Confederate soldiers in Charlottesville that day and the Police just turned the town over to them. The Old Turk and been drinking since he left home and it was a mystery to see how he kept going but he did somehow. After they got off the train they went straight to a saloon so he could get a drink. Dr. Everette happened to be in the saloon and he told The Old Turk "Don't give that boy anything drink". It was Emmett's first trip away from home and he would remember it for the rest of his life.

The morning that the Old Turk came to Glenthorne to work he led the most motley crew that anybody ever saw anywhere on this earth. To see him riding along on his old poor horse with one leg missing and his crutches in his lap. Not long out of the Confederate army with every ambition killed and every hope lost. He was followed by his three small boys on foot behind with three colored men of various sizes and ages all with their hilling hoes on their backs was a dismal sight. Yet he was ambitious, proud, energetic and full of hope and plans for the future.

The Old Turk would say with a sweep of his arms that he expected to live to see the day that his boys would own all of Rockfish as far as he could see. To think that what that meant then staggers the imagination, and yet he lived to see nearly all of his prophecies come true.

Even then as small boys, they knew how to work field hands. Their field hands were paid twenty-five cents a day and they would get five dollars' worth of work out of them. Those boys did not send hands into the field to work, they got in the lead row and said follow me. It was a race all day long without ever looking up or stopping at the ends of rows. When they got to the end they wheeled right into the next row and kept this up til dark.

There was an old man there at Wintergreen who went through the war with The Old Turk and they were close in most of the battles together. He said that The Old Turk was always in the front of battle doing his duty. That is the best you can say for any man "He saw his duty and did it". The Old Turk also did his duty as a civilian. The Old Turk rented and raised his family at Glenthorne and one of his sons bought and turned it into one of the most beautiful and profitable farms in the Valley. It is still in operation today and is farmed by a descendant of The Old Turk.

Visit with HAWES COLMAN at THE WINTERGREEN CEMETERY

When I retired in 2013, I was looking about for something to keep me busy as I didn't want to spend my time not being productive. I had been told by a man almost 100 years old that keeping busy was the secret to a long life.

There is a beautiful cemetery site just east of the Old Wintergreen plantation house. It is the burial site of Hawes Coleman, the founder of Wintergreen Plantation and an ancestor of mine. In 2013 it had not been kept clean of brush and weeds for years. It was surrounded by a stone wall and the Harris family had built a wall for the Harris family next to and connected to the Coleman wall. There was a slave cemetery just east of the Coleman Cemetery. None of these cemeteries had been worked on for many years. Cleaning it up seemed the right thing to do and would be a good use of my time.

I started to go up there one or two days a week spending the entire day. Working in the hot sunshine like that makes you tired and thirsty. Every so often I would sit down against the wall and have a cold beer before a little nap. Despite the work, it was a fairly relaxing way to spend the day. It was sure a peaceful place to sit and contemplate how I have spent my life.

It was right after the Fourth of July I was up there and it was a really hot day. At noon I got my lunch and the ice bag with beer and sat against the wall. After eating and drinking a couple or three beers it was time for a little nap so I drifted off to sleep.

I don't know how long I slept but I became half awake and had an odd feeling that I wasn't alone. I opened my eyes and looked over by the corner of the Harris wall. An old man was sitting there leaning back against the old pine tree with his hat pulled down over his eyes. I thought he was asleep. I thought to myself "Who could that be?". I had never seen anyone up there before and he didn't look familiar. He had long white hair and a beard. His hat and clothing were old and worn. None of it looked like it was from this century.

I looked at him for a while and he didn't move so I said "Hey Mister, are you right?' He pushed his hat back on his head and said "Course I'm alright. Just getting some fresh air and quiet time. That damn Harris crowd buried next to us is always cussing and fighting. A body can't get any rest at all. My wife was a Harris and she is always getting insulted when I talk bad about her family, but there is nothing good I can say about that gang of hellions. The sad thing is they're all ghosts and can't hurt each other. Anyway, who are you? and why are you bothering my rest?"

I didn't know what to do so I introduced myself. Here's this guy waking and up telling me he is a spirit and how unhappy he is with his grave mates. I say "I understand complaining about unruly neighbors but could you back up a bit and tell me who you are."

The old man took his hat off, leaned back, and says. "You are not sleeping and dreaming. I am the old Hawes Coleman that came up here and built Winter Green after the War against England for our Independence. It was long ago and I very rarely talk to a living person but I wanted to thank you for cleaning up our graveyard and showing respect for the dead. Our family seems to have forgotten us you are one of the few who think about us."

I haven't seen him since but every time I go up there, I

find something out of place or a strange feeling in the air. I know he is there and watching everything I do.

The Grand Rally

The late summer days were warm but not hot and the nights began to have that chill in the air that is peculiar to Virginia at this time of the year, the forerunner of autumn, lazy, carefree days, watermelon time.

Where the Adial Road crossed the Rockfish River on the left was the Colored Church Mount Eagle. People had been wending their way all morning along the country roads and paths to attend the Grand Rally. It was the time of year when the Colored People hold their revival. It was the time of year when frying size chickens make that peculiar noise in their throats at night when strange footsteps approach their coops as if they suspect that everything is not just right. The revival usually started at about ten o'clock in the morning and lasted till midnight. It is a continuous performance of preaching, singing, praying, shouting, and drinking. Everyone is free to come and leave as they please.

About a quarter mile from the church, you could see the smoke curling up in long blue spirals in the hazy air from the still where Old Man John Crawford was making brandy out of permanent sweetened apples for John Gannaway, a large red-faced, good-natured Irishman who brought the art of making brandy to Wintergreen.

John Crawford was known far and wide as the best brandy maker in Nelson County. He was also well known as having belonged to William Crawford who ran for President in 1824 during slavery days. John was very proud of having belonged to William Crawford.

Uncle Albert was a tall thin old man who made regular trips to the still about every hour and a half from the meeting to the still where John Crawford would give him a singling of Brandy until he got pretty full. On the last trip after sunset, John Crawford banked the fire under the still and went with Uncle Albert back to the church. John Crawford was a good Christian and a deacon at the Elk Hill church but he liked his drink.

After John Crawford and Uncle Albert got back to the church they sang awhile and preached awhile until late at night. Toward the end, the Paster of the church, Uncle Reuben Loving called on Uncle Albert to pray. By this time Uncle Albert was feeling really good thanks to Gannaway's apple brandy. Uncle Albert got down on his knees and prayed and prayed until the congregation began to get restless. They began to glance around at Uncle Albert on his knees but did not know what to do to stop him as all the men were afraid of him. After a while, the nonstop praying began to be unbearable and something had to be done to stop Uncle Albert from praying all night. John Crawford came up with the answer. He stood up and started to sing. Uncle Albert prayed louder and John Crawford sang louder and louder. All at once the congregation stood up and started to sing with John Crawford singing until they were making so much noise that Uncle Albert could not hear himself pray. Uncle Albert all of a sudden jumped up and said "Take Here, Take Here, let me out of here, the devil is in this Church. Here I am down on my knees praying and John Crawford commences to singing like a fool.

Uncle Albert was a kind of renegade among the colored people, he only went to church in the summertime when they had their big meetings and always had plenty to eat. He used to say that he was a summertime Christian and a wintertime devil but on account of his age, they had to show him some respect.

HENRY RITTENHOUSE WAR Stories

Henry Rittenhouse had served in the War and every so often he liked to tell stories about the War. His company was at the Battle of Fisher's Hill and had been forced into retreat. The company had been running all day and had stopped to rest. When they sat down Henry dropped off to sleep. When he woke up, he could see the heads of his company going out of sight over a hill some distance from him. Henry started running and the Yankees started shooting at him like he was a rabbit. He stopped and threw down his gun and knapsack to surrender but then he thought that he would rather die there than in a Yankee prison. He picked up his gun and knapsack and started to run again and the Yankees started shooting again. He ran into a board fence and started to climb over it. The Yankees shot the fence to pieces under him but he didn't get hit. He finally outrun the Yankees and caught up safely with his company.

Henry would tell the story about John Meeks from up on Stoney Creek that was in his Company. He said that one day the Yankee Cavalry charged them and had their lines all cut to pieces and the Yankees were riding back and forth cutting everybody that could reach with their sabers. A Yankee raised his saber to cut down John Meeks. Henry saw the self-satisfied look on the Yankees' face as he was about to make the killing stroke, but John Meeks ducked his head and threw up his gun. The Yankee's saber slashed the gun but did no harm. John Meeks brought his gun up to the Yankee's breast. The Yankee dropped his gun and threw up his hands in surrender. John Meeks pulled the trigger. The Yankee fell off his horse dead. Such are the fortunes of war but Henry always wondered if John Meeks should have killed this Yankee. John Meeks said that the Yankee had his try and lost. John had his try and won.

During the Battle of Fishers Hill during a strategic retreat Henry was wounded in the leg and was down between the lines. The bullets were thick from both sides. John Meeks noticed that Henry was down with a leg wound. John ran out to where Henry was on the ground with bullets flying thick and fast. Jon gathered henry up on his shoulder and got him back to the Confederate's lines and got him behind some fence rails so that he would not be too exposed to fire from both sides as it would be some time before they could get him to an operating table. John Meeks went out that night and stole an old hen and cooked it to make soup for Henry. After that Henry always had a soft spot in his heart for John Meeks. Whenever John Meeks came around after the was Henry had time for him and he would leave with a bushel of corn and some meat.

John Meeks was a hero and in a modern war, he would come home with a chest full of medals. After that battle at Fishers' Hill, he fought all the way to Richmond and to Appomattox. After the surrender, his gun was taken and he was told to walk home back to Wintergreen. When he finally got back to Wintergreen, he had somehow acquired a Yankee rifle, pistol, and horse. John was not a good worker nor a farmer but he was one hell of a soldier.

John Meeks was my Mother's Uncle.

Viola (Turner) Taylor

Viola was the descendant of slaves owned by the Coleman family at Wintergreen Plantation. Viola lived her entire life at Wintergreen and she was one of the happiest people I have ever known. Though she was always poor she always had a smile and was ready to pitch in and help anyone who needed it.

Viola and her husband Reverend Turner lived in a log cabin about a quarter mile behind Elk Hill, close to the Elk Hill colored graveyard. The Reverend Turner preached in the Old Elk Hill colored church and the New Elk Hill colored church when they moved to the old school house across the river from Glen Thorne. The Reverend Turner passed away before I was born. All the Colored Folks said that he was a real fire and brimstone. Everyone agreed that if he preached your funeral, he may not get you into heaven but he would get you an interview with Saint Peter.

After Reverend Turner passed, Viola had a hard time. The Ewing family who owned Elk Hill let her stay in the cabin with her son and two daughters. She was a good worker and was always in demand during peach and apple season. She could pick fruit from a ladder and was also adept in the packing sheds. When some families needed help with work in the home, Viola was the one they called on.

I always looked forward to her coming to our house to help my mother with canning and preserving the hog meat after slaughtering. It was a big job and served a great need. She was paid and also got a share of the pork and canned vegetables. The best thing about Viola was she loved little children and paid a great deal of attention to me when she came to our house

Viola liked to have a little drink of home-made or so when she could get it. On one occasion my mother had to go somewhere and when she got back, I was out in the yard playing and Viola was not to be found.

My mother finally went upstairs and Viola was in my bed asleep. When my mother woke her up, it was evident that Viola had had a bit to drink. My mother always made a five-gallon jug of blackberry wine to anoint the fruit cake and have it for Christmas. Viola had found the jug in the closet under the hall stairs and had a few drinks. It was so funny my mother couldn't be upset with her. They had known each other since they were children.

After a few years of widowhood, Viola married Bob Taylor who lived down in Nellysford, across from the Rockfish Valley Baptist Church. She still worked and helped the families around Wintergreen. I will always remember her as a happy lady who seemed satisfied with her lot in life.

When I grew up and went into the Service, I remembered coming home and seeing her around Nellysford or helping my mother. She acted toward me as if I was still a little boy and she was watching me to make sure I didn't get into trouble. I miss her.

Appendix: Photographs and Illustrations

UNITED STATES GOVERNMENT

Memorandum

DEPARTMENT OF TRANS
UNITED STATES COA

DATE: 5 Sept 86

SUBJECT: USCG LIGHT STATION MONTAUK POINT DISESTABLISHMENT CEREMONY

FROM: Officer in Charge, Coast Guard Light Station Montauk Point

TO: Commander, Coast Guard Group Shinnecock

    1. USCG Light Station Montauk Point Disestablishment Ceremony

    1255 Station personnel forms at attention

    1300 Attention to trooping of the colors

    OIC welcomes guest and introduces chaplain to give the invocation

    Inspection party inspects station personnell

    OIC introduces guest speakers

    Captain A. J. Tayler, USCG, CO Support Center New York

    Judith Hope, East Hampton Town Supervisor

    LT D. P. Pekoske, USCG, CO, CG Group Shinnecock

    Francis Wyatt
    Reads
    <u>From Montauk Point</u> by Walt Whitman

    BM1 W. Gene Hughes, USCG, OIC Light Station Montauk Point

    Mrs. Peggy Joyce, President Montauk Historical Society

    OIC introduces chaplain to give benediction

    Retire colors

                      W. G. HUGHES

The Officer in Charge of
U.S. Coast Guard Station Montauk Point
request the pleasure of your company at the
Ceremony to Disestablish
U.S. Coast Guard Light Station Montauk Point
at which
Boatswaine Mate First Class W.Gene Hughes
will entrust the Montauk Historical Society
with responsibility for the future guardianship of
Montauk Point Lighthouse
on Friday, the Twelth of September
at one o'clock at U.S. Coast Guard Light Station
Montauk Point

Uniform
Participants - Full Dress Blue
Military Guests - Tropical Blue Long
Civilian Guests - Informal

R.S.V.P.
(516) 668 - 2544

```
FOR OFFICIAL USE ONLY                          DUTY SECTION:  THREE
NOT TO BE REMOVED FROM THE SHIP                DUTY DIVISION: "OPS"

                 U.S.S. SUFFOLK COUNTY (LST-1173)
                        PLAN OF THE DAY
            ALL HANDS ARE HELD RESPONSIBLE FOR COMPLIANCE
                     SUNDAY, 30 OCTOBER 1966

CDO: LTJG KESSLER                              UNIFORM OF THE DAY
DUTY YN: VALIGURA, SN                          OFFICER'S AND CPO'S:
                                               Tropical White Long
                                               OTHER ENLISTED:
                                               Tropical White Long
                                               MARINES:  Tropical Khaki
((((((((((((((((((((((((((((((((((((((((((((((((((((((((((((((((((((((((((
0700  Reveille
0715  Early breakfast
0730  Four hand working party sweep down pier
0745  Muster on station
0800  Turn to.  Titivate ship
1000  Liberty commences for sections one and two
1700  Muster the duty fire party
 30   Shore patrol muster on the quarterdeck
)))))))))))))))))))))))))))))))))))))))))))))))))))))))))))))))))))))))))))
 TES:
 .  Liberty expires as follows:
       E-1 thru E-4 - 0100
       E-5 and above - 0200

2.  No personnel will be permitted to operate any two wheeled vehicles such
as motorbikes, motor scooters or motor cycles during this deployment.

3.  The ship's store will be open today from 1200 until 1300 and will be
closed Monday through Wednesday next week for inventory.

4.  The "Lucky Seven" in San Juan has contributed all known cases of VD
on this cruise.  In addition, various other unsanitary and unhygenic
conditions exist there.  Proceed at your own risk.

5.  Steam will be secured all day today in order to clean the boiler.

6.  A list of divine services in the area is posted on the bulletin
board outside the ship's office and on the quarterdeck.

                              B. F. GESSNER, LT, USN
                              EXECUTIVE OFFICER
```

179

KEEPER OF THE LIGHT, Boatswain's Mate First Class W. Gene Hughes, inspects the antique lens atop the Montauk Point Lighthouse. The last bulb, which has a range of 19 miles when magnified by the lens, lasted a year before it burned out. Mr. Hughes keeps it on his desk. *Eric Kuhn*

The Star Goes To:

The Pre-Automation Light

AS FAR EAST as one can go in New York State, Montauk Point once stretched almost 200 feet farther into the sea. This picture was taken in February, 1889, when Turtle Hill still looked like a turtle. The Coast Guard intends to automate the Light this summer and lease the historic site, which the Montauk Indians called "Womponamon," or "to the east."

DEPARTMENT OF TRANSPORTATION
UNITED STATES COAST GUARD

MAILING ADDRESS
Commanding Officer
USCG Station
New York, NY 10004

1500
15 July 1977

From: Commanding Officer, USCG Station New York
To: BM2 W. Gene HUGHES, USCG
Via: Executive Petty Officer, USCG Station New York

Subj: SAR Boat Coxswain Qualification; certification of

Ref: (a) U. S. Coast Guard Regulations (CG-300)
(b) Small Boat (SAR) Training Program (CG-313)
(c) CGSTA NY INST 3121 (series)
(d) CGSTA NY INST 1540 (series)
(e) Your ltr 1500 dtd 15 July 1977 .

1. Having successfully completed the required course of instruction and having passed the final operational examination for certification as SAR Boat Coxswain at Coast Guard Station New York, you are hereby designated a qualified SAR Boat Coxswain on the following boats assigned to this station;

a. 40' UTB
b. 32' PWB
c. 41' UTB
d. 30' UTB
e. 25' UCB

2. This certification will remain in effect as long as you are performing the duties of Boat Coxswain at Coast Guard Station New York on a continuing basis unless sooner terminated by the Commanding Officer.

3. You shall perform your duties in the manner prescribed by references (a) thru (d) and will acknowledge receipt of this certification hereon.

4. A copy of this certification will be forwarded to Commander, Coast Guard Group New York for inclusion in your service record.

T. C. EISENZAHL

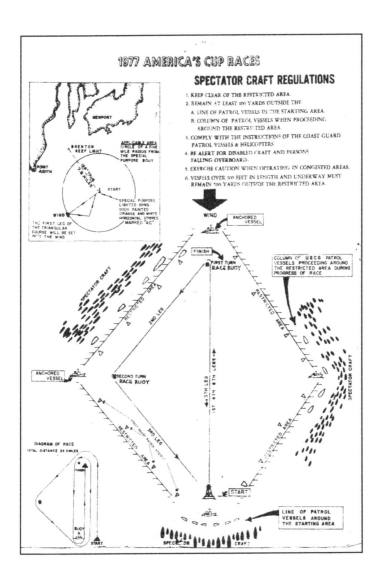

1977 AMERICA'S CUP RACES

SPECTATOR CRAFT REGULATIONS

1. KEEP CLEAR OF THE RESTRICTED AREA.
2. REMAIN AT LEAST 100 YARDS OUTSIDE THE
   A. LINE OF PATROL VESSELS IN THE STARTING AREA.
   B. COLUMN OF PATROL VESSELS WHEN PROCEEDING
      AROUND THE RESTRICTED AREA.
3. COMPLY WITH THE INSTRUCTIONS OF THE COAST GUARD
   PATROL VESSELS & HELICOPTERS.
4. BE ALERT FOR DISABLED CRAFT AND PERSONS
   FALLING OVERBOARD.
5. EXERCISE CAUTION WHEN OPERATING IN CONGESTED AREAS.
6. VESSELS OVER 100 FEET IN LENGTH AND UNDERWAY MUST
   REMAIN 500 YARDS OUTSIDE THE RESTRICTED AREA.

DEPARTMENT OF TRANSPORTATION
UNITED STATES COAST GUARD

MAILING ADDRESS
COMMANDER
FIRST COAST GUARD DISTRICT
150 CAUSEWAY STREET
BOSTON, MASS. 02114

SPECIAL LOCAL REGULATIONS FOR THE 1977 AMERICA'S CUP RACES, NEWPORT, R. I.

These regulations are issued to provide control over the America's Cup Races and to insure safety of life and property in the race area. (Authority 14 USC 89, 46 USC 454, and 33 CFR Part 100). Penalties up to $500 for violation of these regulations may be awarded (46 USC 457). Enforcement will be by U.S. Coast Guard Vessels and helicopters.

1. <u>Effective period</u>: These regulations are effective 0900 until the conclusion on each race daily commencing on 13 September 1977 and on each day thereafter that a race is conducted until the completion of the regatta.

2. <u>Applicable Area</u>: These regulations are applicable within a 5 mile radius of the special purpose lighted ball buoy, painted orange and white horizontally banded in approximate position 7.8 miles bearing 136 T (150.5 M) from Brenton Reef Light (C&GS Chart 1210 NO. 13218). This area is indicated on the chartlet on the reverse hereof.

3. <u>Race Course and Restricted Area</u>: The triangular race area will be marked by the foregoing special purpose buoy and two large inflatable buoys. The race will start at the special purpose buoy with the first leg oriented directly into the wind and follow the course diagram indicated on the reverse hereof. The diamond shaped restricted area around the race course will be marked by anchored vessels and roving U.S. Coast Guard Patrol boats.

4. <u>Spectator Craft</u>: All spectator craft and other vessels operating in the area within five (5) miles of the special purpose buoy shall:

A. Keep clear of the restricted area. Official Press and participating racing syndicate vessels are the only non-Coast Guard craft allowed in the restricted area. These privileged vessels will be identified by the special flag they will be flying.

B. Prior to the start of the race, remain at least 100 yards to the leeward of the line of patrol vessels.

C. Remain at least 100 yards outside the column of patrol vessels when proceeding around the restricted area.

D. Vessels over 100 feet in length and underway must remain 500 yards outside of the restricted area.

E. Comply with the instructions of the U. S. Coast Guard patrol vessels and helicopters. Small patrol boats will be equipped with sirens/horns and flashing blue lights.

F. Be alert for disabled craft and persons falling overboard.

G. Exercise caution when operating in congested areas. Be aware of your wake at all times.

5. Mariners are advised to monitor Channel 22 VHF-FM (157.1 MHZ) for informational broadcasts by the U. S. Coast Guard and any other special conditions that may exist during the course of the race.

W. S. SCHWOB
Rear Admiral, U.S. Coast Guard
Commander, First Coast Guard District

**U.S. Department
of Transportation**

**United States
Coast Guard**

Commanding Officer
USCG TRACEN Cape May

Cape May, NJ 08
Tel: FTS 480-50

18 May 1987

From: Commanding Officer, USCG TRACEN Cape May
To: BM1 1/2 Wilbur G. Hughes 227 60 2606, USCG

Subj: ORDERS FOR INSTALLATION INTO THE RANK OF CHIEF PETTY OFFICER

1. On Wednesday 20 May 1987 at 0630 you will present yourself
to the CPO Mess on board the USG TRACEN Cape May.

2. You will be dressed to resemble a baby and your attire will
include the following accessories:

    a. A Diaper
    b. A T-shirt with baby written on the front
    c. A baby bonnet
    d. Foot attire will consist of booties with bells
    e. A pacifier
    f. A rattle
    g. A baby bottle
    h. Baby blanket

3. You will also have with you:
    a. Two dozen eggs
    b. One box of "Good" cigars
    c. Two large bags of potatoe chips
    d. A dress uniform minus collar devices
    e. Three boxes of Stove Top Turkey Stuffing
    f. 100 dollars in small bills

4. You will be expected to know the lyrics to the following songs:

    a. Rock-A Bye Baby

    b. Yes Sir, I'm your baby

    c. Baby I need your loving

5. Anything else you may wish to have with you is permissible as
long as these minimum requirements are met and you must be able to
carry everything you bring.

6. MUCS Ethridge is directed to supervise your activities until 1300
at which time you are directed to report to the CPO Club on board
TRACEN where you will be tried for your competency as a BM1 1/2
to determine if you are worthy of assuming the status of a
Chief Petty Officer in the United States Coast Guard.

W. L. PRITCHARD
Acting

UNITED STATES COAST GUARD

THIS IS TO CERTIFY THAT
THE COMMANDANT OF THE UNITED STATES COAST GUARD
HAS AWARDED THE

COAST GUARD COMMENDATION MEDAL

TO
WILBUR G. HUGHES
BOATSWAIN'S MATE FIRST CLASS
UNITED STATES COAST GUARD
FOR
OUTSTANDING ACHIEVEMENT
FROM JULY 1983 TO SEPTEMBER 1986

GIVEN THIS 29th DAY OF AUGUST 19 86

G. D. PASSMORE
Rear Admiral (Lower Half), U. S. Coast Guard
Commander, 3rd Coast Guard District
For the Commandant

Keeper Says Lighthouses Fading Out

By The Associated Press

MONTAUK POINT, N.Y. — The keeper of a lighthouse that President George Washington commissioned 190 years ago says his profession is in danger of extinction.

"There are only 37 manned lighthouses left in the States and 37 lighthouse keepers, so we're kind of a dying breed," Coast Guard Petty Officer W. Gene Hughes said.

"It's sad, but there's not much call for people like us," the self-admitted adventurer said from his office in the historic lighthouse that overlooks Land's End.

Hughes, 38, recently experienced one of the thrills of his career when he rode out Hurricane Gloria and its 100-mph winds from inside the 108-foot lighthouse, which has 8-foot-thick walls.

"I like being where the action is," he said, his voice nearly drowned out by the pounding surf on the bluffs below.

In 1966, at the start of his Coast Guard career, Hughes rode Hurricane Inez out on a cutter off Haiti. "It got pretty rough out there, but being at sea was better than being on land in that case."

In Hurricane David in 1979, he cranked a generator that ran the beacon at the Jupiter Inlet Lighthouse for 18 hours in case someone needed haven on the Florida Intercoastal Waterway.

The eye of David, which smashed into land near Palm Beach, Fla., passed over the lighthouse "and everything became deathly still," Hughes recalled.

"It was the strangest experience. The water was like a mirror ... I could hear animals scurrying through the trees, rabbits, squirrels and all of a sudden in 10 minutes it started up again like a freight train coming through."

The native Virginian plans to retire in two years, after he finishes his four-year stint as officer-in-charge of the lighthouse. He said his is not a job for those who cringe when nature goes wild.

"We're the last ones ever to evacuate (during storms)," he said. "That's our job — to stick it out when it gets bad."

It got bad Sept. 27, when 100-mph winds swept eastern Long Island, causing $215 million in damage to property, trees and utility poles.

The lighthouse, one of the nation's oldest, suffered $4,000 in damage when 14 storm windows were blown out, a front porch support toppled and a skylight shattered, Hughes said.

Was Hughes frightened? Did he fear for the safety of his wife and 3-year-old son, who live in an 1860 dwelling beside the lighthouse?

"No, I figured if the lighthouse had been sitting here nearly 200 years, we'd be all right."

189

THE COMMANDANT OF THE UNITED STATES COAST GUARD
WASHINGTON 20593

30 September 1983

From: Commandant
To: BM1 Wilbur G. HUGHES 227 60 2606, USCG

Subj: Letter of Commendation

1. I note with pride and am pleased to commend you for your performance of duty while serving as Executive Petty Officer, Coast Guard Station, Islamorada, Florida from 21 September 1979 to 1 June 1983. During this period you developed and maintained liaison with other federal, state and local law enforcement agencies which resulted in the seizure by Station Islamorada crews of more than one dozen vessels with 78,350 pounds of marijuana. Your efforts also led to the discovery of hidden compartments for carrying contraband. Additionally, you actively coordinated a SAR training program with the local Coast Guard Auxiliary Flotilla, which increased the Flotilla's ability to respond. Your demonstrated professionalism and leadership were consistently noted by District and Group personnel who awarded overall ratings of excellent during inspections.

2. You are commended for your outstanding performance of duty. By your meritorious service you have upheld the highest traditions of the United States Coast Guard.

3. You are hereby authorized to wear the Commandant's Letter of Commendation Ribbon Bar.

D.C. THOMPSON
Rear Admiral, U.S. Coast Guard
Commander, Seventh Coast Guard District
By direction of the Commandant

Certificates of Recognition in his four crossing of the Equator and Imternational Date Line.

30,000 pound seizure of drugs off our US Coast

A visit from the Vice-President of the United States

Wirt and Maggie Hughes

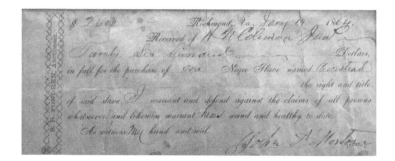

Cost of slave at Winter Green Plantation

JOHN JAY COLEMAN I
1797 – 1869

Maggie Hughes, Robert's mother

Peter Davis with unknown person

Gene with Andy Hickman 1962

ABOUT THE AUTHOR

Gene W. Hughes was born on Spruce Creek Road, Wintergreen in Nelson County, Virginia. His parents were Doris Marshall Hughes and Tucker Hughes. He lived and grew up in the home that his Grandfather Alexander T. Hughes built around 1890. Along with his brothers, Clay and Grady, he attended the old Rockfish Elementary and Nelson County public schools until he entered the military at 18 years of age.

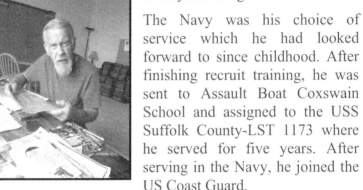

The Navy was his choice of service which he had looked forward to since childhood. After finishing recruit training, he was sent to Assault Boat Coxswain School and assigned to the USS Suffolk County-LST 1173 where he served for five years. After serving in the Navy, he joined the US Coast Guard.

His service included a tours of duty aboard the CG Cutter Glacier in Antarctica, Sylt, Germany and New York City.

Before retiring he completed assignments as Officer in Charge and Company Commander at the Jupiter Light House, Islamorada SAR Station, Florida and the Montauk Light House on Long Island, New York.

After returning home Gene applied for a job at the U. S. Army National Ground Intelligence Center in Charlottesville where he retired again after 23 years as an Army Civilian Employee, giving him 43 years of

Government Service. A very long road for a Spruce Creek Mountain Boy who finally came home from the sea.

July 4th, 11-3pm: Old Wintergreen Day at Spruce Creek Park

While originally scheduled for May 2nd, Old Wintergreen day has been moved to July 4th. Watch for further announcements. Gene Hughes, pictured left, is co-chair of the applicable committee and has been recently chosen as Wintergreen Historian by the RVF Board. Hear what Gene has to say about Old Wintergreen Day:

"The area we call Old Wintergreen with its commercial enterprises was the business and social center for the surrounding area from the end of the Revolution until the 1950s. There were two grist mills, a store, a sawmill, and four distilleries with a magistrate to keep the peace. The Fourth of July 2021 will be the third celebration of Old Wintergreen Day. This is a Sunday afternoon when it was a tradition for the old folks to gather after church and sit on the front porch all afternoon telling stories and having a good time. There will be storytelling, displays, living history, food trucks, and music. The Fourth is our most important Patriotic Holiday. Come on down to old Wintergreen at the intersection of Rt. 151 and Glenthorne Loop at the Rockfish Valley Foundation to celebrate."

Gene now spends most of his time reading, walking the woods, and conversing with the spirits at the family cemeteries around Winter Green. He also volunteers at the Rockfish Valley Foundation and oversees the Foundation's Old Winter Green History Days began by him in 2018. Gene is a member of the All American Honor Guard which does Military Living History from colonial days to the present and marches in local parades.

Gene maintains that the two best decisions that have affected his life were when his ancestors left Jamestown they stopped at Spruce Creek and never thought of moving further West or North and the fact that he had the good sense to join the Navy/Coast Guard instead of the Army.

Today, he is a distinguished and self-proclaimed story-teller, keeper and caretaker of the Coleman, Harris, Davis, Marshall, Dameron and Hughes family graveyards, and a carver and collector of wooden objects and antique metal things found or bought at locations along the old Wintergreen-Rockfish Valley Highway.

He is also an author, planner and host for the past "Old Winter Green Days" festival scheduled for Sunday October 11, 2020 and July 4th, 2021. The next one will be coming in spring or summer 2022.

For more information contact him at email: gene.hughes@nccwildblue.com

W. Gene Hughes